The Cambridge Introduction to
James Joyce

James Joyce is one of modern literature's most important authors, yet those coming to his work for the first time often find it difficult to grapple with. This introduction provides all the essential facts about Joyce's life and works, and explains the contexts in which he was writing. Eric Bulson also explains in clear language the different critical approaches that have been used in Joyce studies over the last fifty years. All Joyce's major works, including *Ulysses*, *Finnegans Wake* and *Dubliners*, are covered, and Bulson gives many suggestions for further exploration. A guide to further reading is included. Students will find this an accessible introduction to understanding and enjoying Joyce.

ERIC BULSON is Lecturer in English and Comparative Literature at Columbia University.

Cambridge Introductions to Literature

This series is designed to introduce students to key topics and authors. Accessible and lively, these introductions will also appeal to readers who want to broaden their understanding of the books and authors they enjoy.

- Ideal for students, teachers, and lecturers
- Concise, yet packed with essential information
- Key suggestions for further reading

Titles in this series:

The Cambridge Introduction to
James Joyce

ERIC BULSON

CAMBRIDGE
UNIVERSITY PRESS

CAMBRIDGE UNIVERSITY PRESS
Cambridge, New York, Melbourne, Madrid, Cape Town, Singapore, São Paulo

CAMBRIDGE UNIVERSITY PRESS
The Edinburgh Building, Cambridge CB2 2RU, UK
Published in the United States of America by Cambridge University Press, New York

www.cambridge.org
Information on this title: www.cambridge.org/9780521549653

First published 2006

Printed in the United Kingdom at the University Press, Cambridge

A catalogue record for this book is available from the British Library

ISBN-13 978-0-521-84037-8 hardback
ISBN-10 0-521-84037-6 hardback
ISBN-13 978-0-521-54965-3 paperback
ISBN-10 0-521-54965-5 paperback

For Mika

Contents

Preface

James Joyce's reputation precedes him more than most writers. Without even reading a line of his work, throngs of people can confidently tell you that he was the near-blind Irish renegade, wandering exile, and self-obsessed artist who made book-reading unnecessarily difficult. Joyce can be difficult, but he is actually a lot of fun to read. You don't have to be a professional literary critic to enjoy him. In fact, if you give him a first or maybe even a second try, you will find that the rewards are endless and open to everyone.

Tracking down an introduction to Joyce can be pretty tricky. By now there is such a mass of critical studies, guides, and glossaries that it is hard to figure out where you can go for the basics. *The Cambridge Introduction to James Joyce* has been written with this dilemma in mind. It provides some of the Joyce abcs and includes an overview of his life, his contexts, his works, and a brief history of his critical reception. The Life chapter provides a bare bones biographical account of Joyce's wanderings between Dublin, Trieste, Zurich, and Paris. Readers who want a more fleshed-out portrait of the artist are encouraged to consult Richard Ellmann's *James Joyce* and John McCourt's *The Years of Bloom: James Joyce in Trieste, 1904–1920*. In the Contexts chapter, I examine how Joyce's "Irishness," which he explored in his Italian newspaper articles, translations, and lectures, was intimately connected with his own becoming as a writer. The Works chapter is devoted to the individual works (*Dubliners, A Portrait of the Artist as a Young Man, Exiles, Ulysses,* and *Finnegans Wake*). Each section explains the major themes, motifs, characters, and narrative techniques, and offers some possible interpretations that can help guide you along. Readers interested in exploring individual works are encouraged to consult the Guide to Further Reading at the end of the book and, if possible, a more expansive list included in *The Cambridge Companion to James Joyce* (ed. Derek Attridge). In the final chapter, I lay out the history of Joyce's critical reception and some of the major approaches that critics have used to assess the significance of his life and work. I have touched on some of the more influential developments in James Joyce studies while also keeping in mind the many critical reassessments that took place in the 1960s and after.

This introduction comes out of my own study of Joyce over the years and owes a great deal to a long and formidable line of critics. As you will soon discover, reading Joyce is a collective effort, one that will no doubt continue for a very long time. Throughout this introduction I will suggest some possible ways to read Joyce's life and works, but these are by no means exhaustive or definitive. It has been my goal to offer up suggestions about how you might read him. I have done my job if you find that you want to give it a first, second, or third try.

Acknowledgments

This book was made possible by Ray Ryan's generosity, support, and patience. I am grateful to Libby Willis for going through the entire manuscript with a keen editorial eye and a sense of humor. I owe my own Joyce introduction and everything after to Edi Giunta. A million thanks are due to Mike Seidel for being a dedicated mentor and friend. Clive Hart generously gave me Wakean wisdom when I really needed it. Geoff Rector and Mike Malouf provided key suggestions on early drafts. Kent Puckett could always be counted on for sound intellectual advice at a moment's notice. With all things Trieste, I owe a particular debt of gratitude to John McCourt. I have benefited enormously from the support and guidance of Jean-Michel Rabaté, who generously agreed to read and comment on this book from beginning to end. I am forever grateful to my parents for their love and encouragement. I could not have done this without Mika. I dedicate this book to her.

Abbreviations

The following abbreviations, editions, and methods of reference have been used.

CW   James Joyce, *The Critical Writings of James Joyce*. Ed. Ellsworth Mason and Richard Ellmann (London: Faber and Faber; New York: Viking, 1959). Hereafter referred to as *CW.*

D   James Joyce, *Dubliners*. Ed. Terence Brown (New York: Penguin, 1992). Hereafter referred to as *D.*

E   James Joyce, *Exiles*. (London: Jonathan Cape, 1952). Hereafter referred to as *E.*

FW   James Joyce, *Finnegans Wake*. (New York: Penguin, 1999). Hereafter referred to as *FW* and followed by page and line numbers.

GJ   James Joyce, *Giacomo Joyce*. Ed. Richard Ellmann (London: Faber and Faber; New York: Viking, 1968). Hereafter referred to as *GJ.*

JJ   Richard Ellmann, *James Joyce*. (Oxford: Oxford University Press, 1982). Hereafter referred to as *JJ.*

LI, II, III   James Joyce, *Letters of James Joyce*. Ed. Stuart Gilbert and Richard Ellmann, 3 vols. (New York: Viking, 1957–1966). Hereafter referred to as *LI, LII, LIII.*

P   James Joyce, *A Portrait of the Artist as a Young Man*. Ed. Seamus Deane (New York: Penguin, 1992). Hereafter referred to as *P.*

SH   James Joyce, *Stephen Hero*. Ed. Theodore Spencer, revised edn. by John H. Slourm and Herbert Cahoon (London: Jonathan Cape, 1956).

SL   James Joyce, *Selected Letters of James Joyce*. Ed. Richard Ellmann (London: Faber and Faber; New York: Viking, 1975). Hereafter referred to as *SL.*

U   James Joyce, *Ulysses*, 2nd revised edn. Ed. Hans Walter Gabler with Wolfhard Steppe and Claus Melchior (New York: Vintage, 1986). Hereafter referred to as *U* and followed by episode and line numbers.

Chapter 1

Life

Dublin, 1882–1904

James Augustine Aloysius Joyce was born at six in the morning on February 2, 1882. The exact time of Joyce's birth was one of the last things uttered by his father, John Stanislaus Joyce, before dying in December 1931. His son needed the information back in Paris so that an astrologer could properly read his horoscope. Joyce assigned a mystical significance to birthdays for his entire life. He pushed a printer in Dijon so hard to have a copy of *Ulysses* published on his fortieth birthday that Joyce scholars have spent the past eighty years arguing over what the final edition should look like. After slipping into a deep bout of depression while writing *Finnegans Wake*, Joyce considered handing the project over to another Irish writer because they shared the same birthday. Joyce originally planned to publish *Finnegans Wake* on his father's birthday as a token of filial affection. He missed the deadline. An advance copy was delivered to his own doorstep on February 2, 1939: Joyce was fifty-seven years old.

Although born and raised in Cork, John Joyce inherited some money from his father's properties and ended up in Dublin, where he met Joyce's future mother, Mary (May) Jane Murray. Together they had ten children (four sons, six daughters, and three miscarriages), and John Joyce supported his family for the first decade or so with a position as a tax collector. In the early years of the 1880s, the Joyce clan lived comfortably, and John managed to provide for the family. After losing this position and eking out a meager pension that May procured for them, the Joyces went into a long and steady decline, moving dozens of times in and around Dublin, often during the night so that they could avoid paying any back rent.

1

For the first ten years of Joyce's life, he was given an education, vacations, and a series of comfortable suburban addresses in Rathgar and Bray. Joyce, the eldest son, was a handsome and clever boy with pale blue eyes, and his parents showered him with love and affection. He began attending the Jesuit boarding school Clongowes Wood College, some forty miles away from home, in 1888 at the age of six. Within a short time he was at the head of his class. In 1891, Joyce was forced to drop out of the school because his family could no longer afford to pay the tuition. He temporarily attended a Christian Brothers school in 1893 until a stroke of good fortune presented itself. After bumping into Father Conmee, who had given up his position as rector of Clongowes Wood College to become prefect of studies at Belvedere College, John Joyce explained why his eldest son had had to give up on the Jesuits. He walked away from this chance encounter with a promise from Father Conmee that Joyce and his brothers could attend Belvedere free of charge. Joyce was brought back to the Jesuits, and for the next five years he distinguished himself as a diligent student and an independent thinker.

After attending a weekend retreat, Joyce experienced a burst of religious fervor (fictionalized in Chapter 3 of *A Portrait of the Artist as a Young Man*) and even considered entering the priesthood for a short time. This flash of religiosity was followed by an even more powerful rejection, which coincided with his sexual awakening. At about the time he was appointed prefect of the Sodality of the Blessed Virgin Mary (a Jesuit association that performed charitable works) in 1896, he also had his first sexual experience with a prostitute on the way home from the theater one evening. Thus began his more frequent visits with the prostitutes on Montgomery Street. He did not make his renunciation of Catholicism public, but he was in the process of storing up a list of grievances that would eventually find a suitable vent in his fiction. Joyce could not reconcile the Catholic doctrine of bodily repression and guilt with his own emerging physical desires. Having enjoyed the religious and the secular virtues of life, the choice had become clear to him: live a life of guilt and repentance or experience the many pleasures that life has to offer.

At Belvedere, Joyce honed his skills at essay writing and received two prizes for English composition, one for the best essay in Ireland in his grade. He also had a knack for foreign languages, and in addition to studying Latin and French he chose to learn Italian. He worked hard to perfect his essay-writing skills, and he would often ask his brother Stanislaus to throw out a topic on the spot so that he could practice. In his early teens Joyce was a voracious reader. At the age of fourteen, he broke free of any systematic study and began to read whatever he wanted. It was during this time that Joyce also began toying with poetry and drama. He attended the theater regularly and voluntarily wrote up reviews that he would compare with those printed in the newspapers the following day. He wrote a series of prose sketches called *Silhouettes* and sixty or so lyric poems collected under the simple title *Moods*. Several years later, he followed this group of poems with another called *Shine and Dark*. Joyce is not much known for his poetry, largely because it is dwarfed by his monumental achievements in fiction. But it was a necessary step in his development as a writer. He published his first collection of poems, entitled *Chamber Music* in 1907, and a second collection in 1929 entitled *Pomes Pennyeach*. Joyce liked the practice of poetry, though he was unsure whether or not he was seriously cut out for it.

In his final year at Belvedere, Joyce discovered the Norwegian playwright Henrik Ibsen. This discovery cannot be underestimated in Joyce's evolution as an artist. In Ibsen he found a kindred spirit, even if the playwright was more than sixty years his senior and living in Norway. He represented the fierce individualism and artistic integrity that Joyce admired. Ibsen's plays were famously controversial because they reacted against the strict moralism and parochialism that Joyce identified with his own native country. Instead of looking to Irish folklore and legend like William Butler Yeats, John Millington Synge and others involved in the Irish Literary Revival, he was interested in a more cosmopolitan vision for Irish literature that looked outward to European models for its inspiration.

At the age of eighteen, he wrote a piece on Ibsen's *When We Dead Awaken* for the *Fortnightly Review*, one of the most prestigious literary reviews in England. In "Ibsen's New Drama" he celebrated Ibsen's ability to represent the drama of everyday life with a stark, unbending realism. Like Ibsen, he believed that art was a confrontation with, not an escape from, reality. "Life," he boldly asserted, "is not to be criticized, but to be faced and lived" (*CW*, 67). His classmates and peers were impressed by and envious of this rare achievement. Ibsen himself even took the time to thank his young admirer for a "benevolent review" through his English translator, William Archer. With his confidence bolstered by a review and a warm letter from his hero, Joyce decided to try his own hand at writing a play. In the summer of 1900, he wrote a four-act play, *A Brilliant Career*, which he dedicated to his own soul. Looking for some critical advice, he sent the play to Archer, who acknowledged Joyce's talent but thought that the canvas was "too large for the subject" (quoted in *JJ*, 79). Joyce agreed and destroyed the play two years later.

After Belvedere College, Joyce attended University College, Dublin, (1898 and 1902) and graduated with a degree in modern languages (English,

French, and Italian). By this time, his love of foreign authors was well known, as was his penchant for rebelling against the received ideas of his classmates. In 1899, when his friends and peers protested against the production of Yeats's play *The Countess Cathleen* at the Abbey Theater for its anti-Irishness, Joyce refused to sign the petition on the grounds that the artist needs his independence from public opinion. Two years later, he wrote an article entitled "The Day of the Rabblement" condemning the Abbey Theater for producing plays in Irish and restricting itself to Irish subjects. Instead of opening itself up to the world, the Abbey Theater, he believed, was further isolating itself. Even worse, for Joyce, this parochialism was a way of kowtowing to the public taste: "the Irish Literary Theatre must now be considered the property of the rabblement of the most belated race in Europe" (*CW*, 70). When the university magazine rejected his article, he joined forces with another student, who had written an essay on equal status for women at the university. They had their articles printed together in a single pamphlet, which they distributed themselves.

During his university years Joyce was less interested in academic honors than he was in life experience. He was intent on conducting "an experiment in living," as Stanislaus called it, one that drew him further away from the Catholic Church.[1] By this time his faith was seriously in crisis, and he found it increasingly difficult to reconcile his intellectual and spiritual freedom with the control of priests and prelates. Moreover, he refused to repress his physical desires and continued to frequent the brothels in Montgomery Street. By rejecting the Church, he was free to develop a spirituality that was entirely his own making. For the rest of his life, he was fascinated by the rituals of the Church and believed that the artist could transform the experience of everyday life into a spiritual essence through art.

Joyce expressed his more combative views about art and aesthetics in front of the Literary and Historical Society in 1900 and 1902. In these public appearances, he deliberately thumbed his nose at the status quo and chose to discuss topics and writers that he knew would incite arguments. In his first paper, "Drama and Life," Joyce challenged the popular notion that art should have any ethical or moral significance and made matters worse by referencing free-thinking atheists like Ibsen. After delivering his paper, he was roundly attacked by his classmates, who refused to believe that art was above ethics. In an impromptu response he replied to each of their charges. From then on, Joyce's lecture was referred to grandly as his "Ibsen night."[2]

For his second lecture Joyce spoke about the nineteenth-century Irish poet James Clarence Mangan. His brother Stanislaus noted that it was a continuation of his first paper and could easily have been called "Poetry and Life."[3]

To the Irish nationalists, Mangan was a tragic hero, who died young during the Irish famine in the 1840s. Mangan's popularity at the turn of the century was due in large part to Yeats and other Irish revivalists. To an audience comprised largely of Irish nationalists, Joyce discussed the Irish neglect and betrayal of its literary heroes. He downplayed Mangan's role as an Irish patriot and cast him instead as an exile scorned by an ignorant and hostile public.

Joyce graduated from University College, Dublin in 1902 and needed to find a career quickly. By this time, he had become familiar with many of Dublin's literati and managed to marshal the support of Yeats, George Russell, and Lady Gregory. Russell acknowledged that the young man was "as proud as Lucifer," and Yeats noticed his "colossal self-conceit" (*JJ*, 100–01). After reading some of Joyce's epiphanies and poems, Yeats was convinced that he had a "delicate talent" but was not sure whether it was "for prose or verse" (*JJ*, 104). Although Joyce's new literary connections could not land him a stable job, they did help him to get some of his poems published. After enrolling in the University Medical School in Dublin, he involved them in a new and completely illogical career choice: medical school in Paris.

Intending to pursue a medical degree and a writing career, Joyce enrolled in the Faculté de Médecine in Paris. After borrowing left, right, and center, he left Dublin on December 1, 1902. In addition to entertaining and feeding Joyce during his layover in London, Yeats provided him with valuable contacts and Lady Gregory secured him a position as an occasional book reviewer for the *Daily Express*, a pro-English newspaper. William Archer recognized the folly of Joyce's decision and was candid enough to tell him: "It's hard enough by giving lessons all day to keep body and soul together in Paris; and how you can expect to do that, and at the same time qualify as a doctor, passes my comprehension."[4] Joyce nevertheless went ahead with his plans, but he soon realized that his first experiment in living was a failure: he was homesick and poor. To make matters worse, he discovered that he could not even afford the matriculation fees for enrollment, and he was forced to abandon his less than brilliant career as a doctor.

This disappointment did not send him back to Dublin. Instead, he decided to stay on in Paris as long as possible and live off the meager payments he received for book reviews, occasional private English lessons, and sporadic loans from home. He managed to write poems and began compiling a notebook on aesthetics, which would serve as the basis for Stephen Dedalus's monologue on aesthetic theory in *Portrait*. Even with family donations (one of them made possible by selling the rug at home), he could hardly keep himself afloat. During this brief period in Paris, Joyce experienced the bohemian lifestyle, living in the Latin Quarter and reading at the library. It was an experience that allowed him to taste the fruit of independence and made him hungry for a life of exile.

On April 10, 1903 Joyce received a telegram that took him back to Dublin immediately: "Mother dying come home father." He arrived back home with long hair, a small beard, and a Latin Quarter hat and did what he could to help his mother through her illness. Nothing could save May Joyce from her battle with cancer. She died on August 13 at the age of forty-four. Because of their break with the Catholic Church, James and Stanislaus refused to kneel down and pray with her. With her death, the rest of the family came rapidly undone. Joyce acted as though he was impervious to the penury and misery of his home life, but it dramatically conditioned how he would define his relationship to Ireland. Joyce never forgot this image of his victimized mother, and he later "cursed the system" responsible for it (*LII*, 48).

After her death, Joyce was even more listless than before and began drinking heavily. During this period, he befriended Oliver St. John Gogarty (who would later appear in *Ulysses* as the bawdy medical student) and lived with him for a short time in the Martello Tower in Sandycove. But it was also during this period that he began to imagine his future career as a writer seriously. He wrote an essay entitled "A Portrait of the Artist" for a Dublin literary review, *Dana*, which gave him the idea for writing *A Portrait of the Artist as a Young Man*, and continued to write poems, many of which would later be collected in *Chamber Music*. With Russell's help he also managed to publish his first short story, "The Sisters," in the *Evening Telegraph*. It would eventually serve as the opening story in his *Dubliners* collection.

After spotting a reddish-brown-haired girl walking down Nassau Street on June 10, 1904, Joyce's life quickly changed. Nora Barnacle had come to Dublin from Galway City to work as a chambermaid in Finn's Hotel. Joyce was immediately smitten. They met on June 16 and took a walk from Dublin to Ringsend where she "made him a man" (*SL*, 159). At this point in his life, Joyce found what he was looking for: a companion who understood him, someone he could give himself to fully. Within two months of their romance, he wanted something more than tender caresses, and he believed that Nora could fill the absence created by the death of his mother and the break with his best friend, J. F. Byrne, who grew increasingly critical of Joyce's licentious and reckless behavior. In many ways, Nora might not seem like the perfect match for the aspiring artist. She did not share his passion for literature and he quickly realized that she "cared nothing" for his art (*LII*, 73). But whatever she lacked in formal education and refinement, she made up for in beauty, wit, courage, and daring.

Their relationship reached a crisis point after only four months. Because Joyce fiercely rejected the institution of marriage, it would be impossible for them to live together. Instead of letting Ireland come between them, Joyce and Nora decided to leave it behind. They boarded a boat on October 8, separately so as not to arouse suspicion, with only enough money to get to Paris, where they planned to borrow again before moving on to Zurich. After finding out that the position he had been promised at the Berlitz school in Zurich had been filled, Joyce and Nora stopped in Trieste for ten days before moving on to Pola (then under Austro-Hungarian rule), where another Berlitz school had just opened. After only five months, they returned to Trieste in March 1905, and it was here that Signore and Signora "Zois," as they were known to the Triestines, spent the next ten years of their life. During this Triestine decade, Joyce made three return trips to Ireland (two in 1909 and one in 1912), but with each visit it became increasingly clear to him that a life of voluntary exile was a necessary precondition for his becoming an artist.

Trieste, 1904–1915

Situated at the northern tip of the Adriatic Sea, Trieste was a major port for the Austro-Hungarian Empire. It was a bustling cosmopolitan center comprised of Slavs, Italians, Greeks, Austrians, and Hungarians. Despite this diverse collection of nationalities and tongues, everyone spoke Triestino. It was a polyglot dialect made up of Italian, German, Slovenian, Croatian, Czech, Greek, Sicilian, Turkish, and Spanish. Joyce quickly updated the archaic thirteenth-century Italian he had learned when studying Dante with a living language that he would continue to speak with his two children, Giorgio and Lucia, for the rest of his life.

Shortly after arriving in Trieste, Joyce needed to figure out his new role as a family man. He had convinced Nora to follow him on the condition that he could provide for her. Their months in Pola were pleasant enough, but the arrival of their son Giorgio on July 27, 1905 was a powerful reminder of Joyce's family responsibilities. He needed to find a way to support them and write. It was a particularly difficult time for Nora because she did not know Italian or German, and her husband spent a lot of time out drinking.

In July 1906 the family moved to Rome so that Joyce could work in a bank copying out letters. The pay was good enough, but the long hours made it impossible for him to get any writing done. Not long after they returned to

Trieste, their second child, Lucia, was born on July 26, 1907. Throughout the summer, they were seriously poverty-stricken but somehow they managed to get by. During these early years, Joyce's role as a father and husband was constantly clashing with his dreams as a writer. Like the disillusioned Little Chandler in "A Little Cloud," he began to worry that with a wife, children, and a meager salary, "He was a prisoner for life" (*D*, 80).

To support his family Joyce gave English lessons at the Berlitz School. Yet he soon found that his daily expenses far exceeded his earnings. In need partly of financial help and partly of a companion with whom he could discuss his writing, he convinced Stanislaus to come to Trieste. After his arrival in October 1905, Joyce unloaded many of the financial and familial obligations onto his brother. For the next ten years, Stanislaus was counted on at various points to pay for rent, clothing, and food. He was also put in charge of finding the family apartments, rescuing them from sporadic evictions, paying his brother's debts, taking on his brother's English lessons, and monitoring his brother's drinking. It was a role he begrudgingly accepted.

After leaving the Berlitz school, Joyce continued to give private English lessons over the years, but he also came up with more inventive schemes to make a buck. In 1907 he approached Italian newspapers in Trieste and around Italy about writing articles on Irish subjects and approached Italian editors about doing translations of Irish writers. In 1909 he began importing Irish Foxford Tweed from Dublin and sold it to his friends and students. In 1910 he opened the first movie theater in Dublin, the Volta cinema, after putting together an array of investors and lawyers to support his venture. After six months, the project was deemed a "fiasco": sales were low, investors pulled out, and he was never paid for his services. In 1912 he applied for a teaching position at the University of Padua. After taking the oral and written exams, in which he scored very highly, his candidacy was revoked because the university refused to recognize his Bachelor's degree from University College, Dublin. In July 1913 he finally landed a well-paid job at the Scuola Superiore di Commercio "Revoltella" for six hours of teaching a week. The work was not too demanding and Joyce finally received a steady income. For the next two years, the Joyces enjoyed more stability than they had ever had before in Trieste and even remained in the same one apartment (which rarely happened).

When Joyce had first arrived in Trieste, he had published three stories in the *Irish Homestead*, a weekly publication for the Irish Agricultural Organization Society, and book reviews in the *Daily Express*. In these early years he often wondered whether he was really cut out for the literary life. When he received the proofs for *Chamber Music*, he was less than pleased with the results: "I don't like the book but wish it were published and be damned to it. However, it is a young man's book. I felt like that. It is not a book of love verses at all, I perceive" (*LII*, 219). He was more certain of his talents for writing fiction. During the first few years in Trieste, he continued to write stories for *Dubliners* but because of a series of failed negotiations with publishers, who wanted him to alter various passages, it was not published until 1914 (the trials and tribulations of *Dubliners* are discussed more fully in Chapter 3). At the same time, Joyce also continued to work on an autobiographical novel, *Stephen Hero*, which he would rewrite and publish as *A Portrait of the Artist as a Young Man*. Like *Dubliners*, the publication was delayed. *Portrait* appeared in serial form and was published in 1916. He wrote *Exiles* between 1914 and 1915 (published in 1918), and began to work on the first three episodes of *Ulysses* (published in 1922). Although he was, for the most part, unpublished during the Trieste years, he completed a number of projects and amassed ideas for the future. The Trieste decade was, his friend Philippe Soupault later observed, "the most important in all his life."[5]

In Trieste, Joyce was not known as a writer of fiction except among a small coterie of devoted students. Among the Triestines he was the language teacher, Irish journalist, occasional lecturer, and translator. His public persona was best defined in *Il Piccolo*, Trieste's daily newspaper, when, after a series of twelve lectures he delivered on *Hamlet* in 1912 and 1913, he was cast as "a thinker, man of letters, and occasional journalist." Between 1907 and 1912 he occasionally wrote newspaper articles in Italian for *Il Piccolo della Sera* on Irish politics, literature, and culture and delivered lectures in Italian on Ireland, Daniel Defoe, and William Blake (I talk about these more extensively in Chapter 2). Although he was antagonistic to Irish nationalist movements when he was in Ireland, in Trieste he was the self-appointed mouthpiece for the Irish, and he used these public performances to introduce and defend his native country. He also capitalized on the fact that his grievances against the British Empire would find a sympathetic ear with the Italian irredentists, who were waging their own anticolonial struggle against the Austro-Hungarian Empire.

Journalism came easy to him, and after writing his first three articles, he confided to Stanislaus, "I may not be the Jesus Christ I once fondly imagined myself, but I think I must have a talent for journalism. I could scarcely have written for the papers my articles have appeared in, if I hadn't artistic talent but in Dublin I could do nothing."[6] Between 1909 and 1912 Joyce wrote other articles on the victimization of Oscar Wilde (1909), the preachiness of George Bernard Shaw (1909), the defeat of the second (1910) and eventual passing of the third (1912) Home Rule Bill in Ireland, and two lyrical travel pieces on Galway and the Aran Islands (1912).

In December 1913 Joyce's luck began to change. The American poet Ezra Pound, who was then living in London, contacted him at Yeats's behest to see if he wanted to publish any poems or short stories in British and American journals. The pay was modest but the publications would get Joyce's name in circulation. Pound agreed to publish "I hear an army" in his collection *Des Imagistes*. In addition, he thought that *Portrait* was "damn fine stuff" and quickly arranged to have it published serially in *The Egoist*.[7] He also managed to get a few stories from *Dubliners* published in *The Smart Set* and encouraged everyone he knew to read and promote Joyce's work. Over the next decade, Pound was an invaluable supporter. His encouragement, generosity, connections, selflessness, foresight, and dedication were responsible for bringing Joyce out of a publishing rut and into the world.

Just when his life as an artist was starting to look promising, Austria-Hungary declared war on Serbia in July 1914. Life in Trieste became increasingly difficult, and he had no choice but to attend to his more pressing personal circumstances. The Scuola Superiore di Commercio where he was teaching closed in 1915, and many of its students were drafted into the army. That same year, the Austro-Hungarian government interned Stanislaus for supporting the Italian irredentists. Joyce made plans to leave with his family. With the assistance of his most influential friends and pupils, the Joyce clan received travel passes to Zurich. Leaving their furniture and books behind, they boarded a train for Switzerland on June 27, 1915. No one could predict how long the war would last, but Joyce was glad that they would be spending it in a neutral country. "Now that everyone in Trieste knows English," he remarked before leaving, "I will have to move on."[8]

Zurich, 1915–1919; Trieste, 1919–1920

While the war raged across Europe, life in Zurich was quiet but costly. Their financial burden was relieved at first by two grants engineered by Yeats and Pound. Joyce's monetary worries were also allayed by the regular stipends he received from Edith McCormick Rockefeller, who lived in Zurich, and Harriet Shaw Weaver, who chose to remain anonymous back in London. Both women supported his literary endeavors for the duration of the war, and it was through their patronage that Joyce was able to devote all his attention to writing *Ulysses*.

Shortly after his arrival, the last installment of *A Portrait of the Artist as Young Man* appeared in *The Egoist*. He hoped that the success of the serial publication would expedite its publication as a book. A number of publishers decided to pass because of the difficulty they would have finding a wartime audience. In 1916 B. W. Huebsch agreed to bring out an edition of 750 copies in America. Fueled by positive reviews, the first edition sold out by early summer. After the publication of *Portrait*, Joyce began looking for a stage company to put on *Exiles*. Yeats considered it for a time but decided not to. Joyce approached the London Stage Society on two separate occasions without success, then teamed up with Claud Sykes, an English actor, to found an acting troupe, the English Players, with the long-term goal of bringing his own play to the stage. The British Consulate supported their endeavor, believing that a theater company would complement the other conduits of pro-British propaganda in Zurich. Joyce, however, had some Irish intentions for his English Players. For the first play they chose Oscar Wilde's *The Importance of Being Earnest* (1895) because of Joyce's firm belief that "an Irish safety pin is more important than an English epic" (quoted in *JJ*, 423).

Complications soon arose between Joyce and one of the British actors, Private Henry Carr, who claimed that the English Players were responsible for covering the cost of his costume. Joyce refused to reimburse him and made the counterclaim that Carr owed him money for tickets he had sold. The two soon took their dispute to court, where the judge ruled in Joyce's favor over the ticket reimbursement. At the same time, Joyce was also suing Carr for libel. In this case, however, he was not victorious, and the judge ordered Joyce to pay the court costs of 59 francs and damages of 120 francs. He ended up paying 50 francs. Because of Joyce's private battle, the English Players were hassled by the British Consulate, and the officials even threatened to revoke Joyce's British passport (which he kept for the rest of his life even though the formation of the Irish Free State in 1922 meant that he could have applied for an Irish passport). In response, he silently left the company. He subsequently had his revenge on Carr by incorporating him into *Ulysses* as the belligerent Private, who punches Stephen Dedalus in the face and utters the memorable line, "I'll wring the neck of any fucker says a word against my fucking king" (*U* 15: 4598–99).

In 1919 the war ended, and the Joyces planned to return to Trieste. Joyce was grateful for the productive and peaceful years he spent in Zurich and believed that his distance from the tragedy and destruction of the war enabled him to create something for future generations: "I wrote the greater part of the book [*Ulysses*] during the war. There was fighting on all fronts, empires fell, kings went into exile, the old order was collapsing with a crash; and I had, as I sat down to work, the conviction that in the midst of all these ruins

I was building something for the most distant future."[9] Whenever anyone asked Joyce what he did during the war, he replied curtly, "I wrote *Ulysses*."[10]

When they arrived back in Trieste in mid-October, Stanislaus was not pleased. After four years in a detention camp, he had just begun to get his life back in order and knew that he would be thrust into the role of his brother's keeper yet again. The Joyces lived in a one-bedroom apartment together with his sister Eileen (who returned with Joyce in 1910), her husband Frantisek Schaurek (whom she had married in May 1915), their two daughters, Stanislaus, a cook, and a babysitter. What was supposed to be a temporary arrangement lasted nine months. In these cramped conditions Joyce somehow managed to work on *Ulysses*. He also collaborated with Carlo Linati on an Italian translation of *Exiles*, which was published in the Milanese journal *Il Convegno* in 1920.

After the war, life in Trieste, which now belonged to Italy, was expensive, drab, and bleak. For the second time, Pound came to Joyce's rescue. After corresponding for seven years, the two finally met in Sirmione, Italy, in June 1920. Pound persuaded Joyce to move to Paris in order to get *Ulysses* published. Following Pound's advice, he resigned his position at the university, arranging for his brother to take over, and in less than a month, the Joyces left Trieste for the last time. Looking back on his Trieste years, he told a friend, "I cannot begin to give you the flavour of the old Austrian Empire. It was a ramshackle affair but it was charming, gay, and I experienced more kindnesses in Trieste than ever before or since in my life . . . Times past cannot return but I wish they were back."[11]

Paris, 1920–1940; Zurich, 1940–1941

In 1937, after living in Paris for seventeen years, Joyce adjusted the compass of his affections. "In my heart," he remarked to the Polish novelist Jan Parandowski, "Paris is the second city after Dublin."[12] He arrived in Paris in 1920 hoping that he would get three months to finish "*Circe* in peace." He ended up staying there until 1939.

In 1920 money trickled in from the sales of his books, but he owed his financial stability during these years to the patronage of Harriet Shaw Weaver, who first began supporting him in Zurich. She sent her gifts no-strings attached and managed to maintain her anonymity for the first three years. On 6 July 1919 Weaver revealed herself and admitted that her donations were intended to free up his "best and most powerful and productive years" (quoted in *JJ*, 491). From 1917 until his death, Weaver gave Joyce what in today's currency would amount to one million dollars. But she was much more to Joyce than a source of financial stability. She became a critical sounding board as he wrote *Ulysses* and *Finnegans Wake*, and he came to depend on her for intellectual and emotional support.

In Paris the Joyces enjoyed a more cosmopolitan lifestyle, and his friends quickly noticed that he possessed a certainty he lacked in Trieste and Zurich. The Joyces continued speaking Triestino within the family, but they were eager to enjoy the unique culture and sophistication that could only be found in the French capital. Joyce's second stay in Paris was a far cry from his first. He arrived there in 1902 halfheartedly in pursuit of a medical career, but he returned in 1920 as something of a literary celebrity. With the tactical promotion of Pound, his work preceded him, and the community of locals and expatriates were eager to make his acquaintance. As an ingenious advertising stint for *Ulysses*, the poet Valery Larbaud arranged for a séance, which was really a lecture and reading, to be held in Adrienne Monnier's bookshop on December 7, 1921. With more than 250 people in attendance, the night was a great success. Subscriptions poured in and Joyce's novel was poised to become a bestseller. He still had to finish it.

As exciting as the public attention may have been, Joyce also needed to find a publisher. Such a prospect became even more doubtful after customs officials in America confiscated four different chapters of *Ulysses*, which were being serialized in *The Little Review*. With all the talk of "undies" and onanism, the "Nausicaa" episode caught the attention of John Sumner, a secretary of the New York Society for the Prevention of Vice, and the editors, Jane Heap and Margaret Anderson, were called to court. The court case did not raise the kind of publicity that Joyce wanted, nor did it generate any useful verdict regarding his book's alleged obscenity. As their sentence, Heap and Anderson were forced to pay fines of fifty dollars each. The serial publication of *Ulysses* was stopped indefinitely.

Because of the censorship laws in America and England, Joyce began to worry that his novel would never appear. Given the possibility of obscenity charges, no one was willing to risk publishing it, and Joyce, as always, refused to alter or omit a word. Circumstances changed after the American-born bookseller, Sylvia Beach, agreed to bring out *Ulysses* in Paris under the imprint of Shakespeare and Company, the name of her bookstore. She even agreed to an unprecedented contract: Joyce would receive 66 percent of the net profits.

With generous promoters and a contract in place, Joyce revised the earlier episodes and forged ahead with the last three. For Joyce, the revision process was a creative act, and with the mass of notes and drafts he had compiled over the previous seven years, he interwove layers of thematic connections, phrases, words, and allusions that would give his massive tome more unity. For Maurice Darantière, his printer in Dijon, the task of deciphering the extensive emendations and editorial symbols was a complete nightmare. As a result, scores of errors were inadvertently planted throughout the entire first edition. On February 2, 1922 Darantière managed to deliver *Ulysses* warts and all by the Dijon-Paris express just in time for Joyce's fortieth birthday.

Now that Joyce had some time to rest and recover, he impatiently awaited the opinions of his critics. Pound chimed in with enthusiastic reviews, making the claim that "*Ulysses* is, presumably, as unrepeatable as Tristram Shandy."[13] T. S. Eliot declared that *Ulysses* was "the most important expression which the modern age has found."[14] Ernest Hemingway called it a "goddamn wonderful book." Yeats considered it a "work of genius" even if he could not finish it. Gertrude Stein admitted that Joyce was a "good writer" (quoted in *JJ*, 529, 531).

Joyce may have obviated the censors by publishing *Ulysses* in Paris, but it would not last. British Customs officials soon confiscated a copy of *Ulysses* at the Croydon Airport in London.[15] The Director of Public Prosecutions did not read through the entire 732 pages, but he did alight upon the final forty or so from the "Penelope" episode, by far the raciest pages in the book. *Ulysses* was subsequently deemed "obscene and indecent," and the Director refused to allow it into England.[16]

During his year-long hiatus from the labors of *Ulysses*, Joyce mulled over his next project. He joked about writing a "history of the world" and began to sort through the unused notes from *Ulysses*. As was the case with his earlier books, which tended to grow organically out of one another, his next project was no exception. On March 11, 1923 he grandly announced to Miss Weaver: "Yesterday I wrote two pages – the first I have written since the final *Yes* of Ulysses" (*SL*, 296). Because of its immense complexity, coupled with Joyce's continuous eye troubles and the mental illness of his daughter Lucia, *Finnegans Wake* occupied him for the next sixteen years.

Even though Joyce turned his attention to writing another book, he continued to monitor the translation, critical reception, and general promotion of *Ulysses*. During these years, a number of book-length studies were also under way for the careful fashioning of the man and his work (I discuss them more fully in Chapter 4). Joyce encouraged his friend Stuart Gilbert to write a study on the Homeric parallels. Shortly after his success with Gilbert, he approached Herbert Gorman to write his biography. Gorman was an American journalist and novelist who had written the first critical study of Joyce in 1924, and he accepted Joyce's proposal, unaware of the difficulties he would face. Although Joyce was eager to make his life public, he was very guarded about the image he wanted Gorman to project. In 1933 Joyce's friend Frank Budgen volunteered to write a book about the making of *Ulysses* that provides a glimpse into Joyce's personality and compositional methods.

By 1931 Joyce wanted to insure that his personal and private affairs were in place. After twenty-six years together, Joyce and Nora were married on 4 July (his father's birthday) to make their union official under British law. The private service was almost postponed when Joyce announced that the two had already been married in 1904 under false names (*LIII*, 222). This second marriage, if it was one, was needed to ensure that Joyce's estate would be transferred to Nora and the children in the event of his death. It is suspected that Joyce married Nora on his father's birthday as a gesture of atonement for their unwedded departure from Ireland twenty-seven years earlier (*JJ*, 637). But whatever amends he intended to make, he was soon informed that his father had died on December 29. Joyce was devastated by the news, though he would not travel to Dublin for the funeral, and he considered giving up on *Finnegans Wake*. The cycle of life and death that he bemoaned at this moment was eased by the birth of his first grandson, Stephen Joyce, on February 15, 1932.

Another bit of good news reached Joyce after the obscenity trial against *Ulysses* went to the United States District Court in New York in 1933. The trial was presided over by Judge John Woolsey, who actually spent the summer reading the book. Joyce's attorney, Morris Ernst, argued that *Ulysses* was not obscene for its own sake. Rather, it was a literary classic intent on exploring the social and psychic life of human beings. Woolsey sided with the defense, and in his landmark decision declared that "whilst in many places the effect of 'Ulysses' on the reader undoubtedly is somewhat emetic, nowhere does it tend to be an aphrodisiac" (quoted in *JJ*, 667). Joyce was overjoyed with the news. In a brief public statement he told the press through an interlocutor: "Mr Joyce finds the judge to be not devoid of a sense of humour" (*JJ*, 667).

This period of Joyce's life was also characterized by the worsening of Lucia's mental illness. He encouraged her love of dancing, painting, book-binding, and drawing and spared no expense promoting her interests. But he came to identify her illness with his own literary experiments, and it was an identification for which he felt an enormous amount of guilt: "Whatever spark or gift I possess has been transmitted to Lucia, and has kindled a fire in her brain" (*JJ*, 650). By 1936, Lucia's outbursts were impossible to ignore. Joyce could no longer deny the fact that her condition was deteriorating, and Lucia was sent to a sanitarium in Ivry near Paris.

Although this final decade of Joyce's life was darkened by his daughter's illness, his father's death, and his increasing blindness, Joyce continued to write. The composition of *Finnegans Wake* (which I discuss more fully in Chapter 3) did not follow the frenetic pace of *Ulysses*, but sections of it were drafted and revised in fits and starts. As it neared completion Faber and Faber asked Joyce to submit the title that he and Nora had kept secret for sixteen years (the serialized sections were published under the title *Work in Progress*). Before going public with the title, he challenged his friends to guess and promised 1,000 French francs to the winner. With a couple of hints, Eugene Jolas finally cracked the code. The following morning Joyce delivered the prize in ten-franc pieces. *Finnegans Wake* was officially published in England and America on May 4, 1939. Joyce was not very pleased with the reactions. Carefully monitoring the reviews, he noted that only a few managed to "rise above the stupor." Most (Joyce counted more than a hundred in England and America) ranged from dismissive stupefaction to bewildered appreciation.

Joyce's worry that the eruption of another war in September would distract public attention from his book soon came true. In December, he and Nora left Paris for Saint-Gérand-le-Puy in the south of France, where they stayed for a year. When asked what he intended to write next, Joyce responded, "something very simple and very short" (*JJ*, 731). Still exhausted from *Finnegans Wake*, Joyce also complained more frequently of the stomach pains that had begun troubling him several years earlier. Doctors first attributed these pains to nerves but would now soon discover – too late – that he had developed a duodenal ulcer. When the Nazis arrived in June, Joyce and Nora made plans to leave for Zurich. His first request was denied because the Swiss authorities, confusing Joyce with Leopold Bloom, suspected that he was Jewish. With the intervention of friends, however, he obtained the proper papers for himself, Nora, Stephen, and Giorgio. He was unable to secure a permit for Lucia but hoped that he would have a better chance after he arrived in Zurich. Joyce never saw his daughter again.

Joyce, Nora, and Giorgio returned to the city that had first given them refuge during World War I. Several weeks after their arrival, Joyce's stomach cramps worsened and the doctors decided to operate. Although he regained consciousness after the surgery, he soon passed into a coma and died of a perforated duodenum at 2.15 a.m. on January 13, 1941. With a modest ceremony and a few friends, he was buried in Zurich's Fluntern Cemetery two days later. When asked by a Catholic priest if she wanted a religious service, Nora refused: "I couldn't do that to him" (*JJ*, 742). A wreath with a lyre symbolizing Ireland was placed by the graveside. Nora Joyce remained in Zurich until her death on April 10, 1951; she was buried in the same cemetery as her husband but not next to him. The two were disinterred and buried side by side in 1966.

Chapter 2

Contexts

Joyce the modernist

By the time Joyce was twenty-six years old, he had tried out a number of possible career paths without any real success. According to Stanislaus's calculations, his older brother failed as "a poet in Paris, as a journalist in Dublin, as a lover and novelist in Trieste, as a bank clerk in Rome, and again in Trieste as a Sinn Feiner, teacher, and University Professor."[1] He was right on all accounts except one. Joyce "the novelist" had not in fact failed. When Stanislaus made this observation, his brother was in the process of revising *Stephen Hero* into *A Portrait of the Artist as a Young Man*. It was a decision that officially marked his turn away from nineteenth-century naturalism and toward the formal and linguistic experimentation that we have come to identify more generally with literary modernism. If it is not surprising that Joyce became a professional writer, one who enjoyed success in his own lifetime (a rare fate for writers), it *is* surprising that he managed to write the kinds of fiction he did. Nothing quite like *Ulysses* or *Finnegans Wake* existed before and the literary landscape was not the same afterward. Revolutionary thinkers like Joyce do sometimes arrive in the world, and it is through them that an entire age is defined. If we cannot always explain how they become visionaries, we can identify some of the contexts in which they develop.[2] This chapter considers, in particular, Joyce the modernist and looks at his various roles as a journalist, translator, and lecturer in Trieste.

Joyce is regarded as one of the leading high modernists. Although critics are divided about the specific features that define modernism, they are willing to agree that the term identifies much of the visual art, literature, music, dance, and architecture produced between 1890 and 1940. Striving to become modern and in reaction to the accelerated pace of modernity, a number of artists broke with existing modes of representation and there was an increased focus on the city, industry and technology, war, speed, mass markets, and communication. But even within this relatively brief period of time there are marked subdivisions. The modernist timeline can be imagined as a kind of arc that really takes off in the 1910s, peaks in the 1920s, and begins its slow decline in the 1930s. Virginia Woolf identified December 1910 as the moment when "human character changed," and critics have come to regard the decade after as a period of unusual intellectual ferment.[3] The year 1922 is one of those magical years in literary history. It was during this year that such major works of high modernism as Joyce's *Ulysses* and T. S. Eliot's *The Waste Land* (made possible by the editorial genius of Ezra Pound) appeared. Creative rumblings could be heard in the 1910s from these writers, but no one could have predicted just how far their experiments with language and literary form would go. During the 1930s modernist writers such as Eliot returned to more traditional and rigidly defined literary forms or, like Pound and Wyndham Lewis, they became enamored with the fascist politics of Italy and Germany. Joyce is unique partly because he continued to push his experiment even further and kept his distance from the siren-song of contemporary politics.

From the 1910s onward, formal and linguistic experimentation were prized above all else. If literature were going to be distinctly modern, it was necessary, as Pound said, to "make it new." Restricting ourselves to literary modernism, we find that Joyce was in some serious company: Virginia Woolf, Franz Kafka, Wyndham Lewis, Gertrude Stein, Ford Maddox Ford, Djuna Barnes, William Faulkner, Filippo Marinetti, Djuna Barnes, T. S. Eliot, W. B. Yeats, Marcel Proust, Ernest Hemingway, and Alfred Döblin. Even with this abbreviated list, we begin to see how much modernism was an international phenomenon that included poets, playwrights, and novelists from around the globe. Although literature departments today often organize courses on modernism around national divides (Anglo-American, German, Italian, French), these writers saw themselves as belonging to a global network. In cities such as Paris, Florence, Vienna, Prague, London, Berlin, and New York, there was an entire industry of translators, journals, editors, and reviewers, willing to promote "local" writers and distribute them beyond national borders. Throughout his life Joyce capitalized on this expansive network. In one representative instance, he read an Italian review of *Portrait* when living in Zurich, translated it himself, and asked Pound to reprint the new English version in *The Egoist*, a literary magazine based in London.

Although Joyce is considered one of the leading British modernists, he was, of course Irish, and lived in Ireland when it was still part of the British

Empire. I will deal with the more complicated issue of Joyce's "Irishness" in due course, but it is necessary to emphasize that he never belonged to any modernist group. At a time when there were diverse and different movements such as Bloomsbury, the Futurists, Imagists, Vorticists, Expressionists, Surrealists, and Dadaists, Joyce kept his distance. He was always suspicious of groups and fought hard to maintain his artistic independence. So even when we pin the "modernist" label on him or put him in the company of Beckett, Conrad, Woolf, and Yeats, we need to acknowledge that Joyce, like all these others, was a singular creation: an Irishman writing in English as he moved around Europe.

What Charles Baudelaire did for lyric poetry in the nineteenth century, Joyce did for the novel in the twentieth century. He found a way to make literature capture the ephemerality of modern life. The realist novel, which was enormously successful in England and Europe in the second half of the nineteenth century, could no longer adequately represent the reality of a world that had undergone dramatic social, political, and technological upheavals in the first decades of the twentieth century. Yet increased literacy, the rise of mass markets, and the cheaper production and circulation costs for books and journals did not lead to the widespread popularity of modernist literature. For Joyce and so many other writers during this period, formal complexity and obscurity were considered literary virtues that ended up alienating readers. The difficulty of so many modernist texts created a conspicuous divide between intellectuals and the masses.[4]

It is paradoxical perhaps that Joyce put Leopold Bloom, one of the most memorable everymen in literary history, in a book that he would never read. As we know from Bloom's daylong wanderings, he prefers *Tit-Bits* to, say, Tennyson. His literary tastes may not be very refined, but Joyce focuses our attention on the complex workings of his inner life. Using a stream-of-consciousness narrative technique, Joyce gives us unmediated access into Bloom's most private thoughts and sense impressions and paints a humanistic portrait of modern life in the process.

Joyce certainly knew about the work of contemporary writers, but he rarely commented on them directly. This unabashed disinterest infuriated Wyndham Lewis. He took Joyce's reticence as willful condescension. Lewis was the one critic, though, whose negative assessments really got to Joyce. In *Time and Western Man*, he argued that "the schoolmaster in Joyce is in great evidence throughout [*Ulysses'*] pages."[5] Stephen Dedalus, he argued further, was a cliché and Bloom a theatrical Jew. He even complained about the stilted diction of *Portrait*. On the occasions when Joyce decided to issue a comment about another writer, he was reserved, dismissive, or evasive. After glancing over a few pages of Proust, he claimed not to see "any special talent" (*JJ*, 488). When he finally read *A la recherche du temps perdu*, he remarked more generously that Proust "is the best of the modern French writers, and certainly no one has taken modern psychology so far, or to such a fine point."[6] Upon reading *The Waste Land*, he seemed almost surprised to discover that "Eliot was a poet" (quoted in *JJ*, 495). It is not clear if Joyce ever read Woolf, but she had a few unflattering things to say about him. She referred to the early episodes of *Ulysses* as "the scratching of pimples on the body of the bootboy at Claridges."[7] In her essay "Mr. Bennett and Mrs. Brown," she went even further: "Mr Joyce's indecency in *Ulysses* seems to me the conscious and calculated indecency of a man who feels that in order to breathe he must break the windows. At moments, when the window is broken, he is magnificent. But what a waste of energy!"[8] Unlike Woolf, Eliot was genuinely dazzled by Joyce's achievement, particularly in regard to *Ulysses*, and told her in confidence that "the book [*Ulysses*] would be a landmark because it destroyed the whole of the nineteenth century. It left Joyce himself with nothing to write another book about. It showed up the futility of all English styles."[9]

Joyce's influence on later writers was immense and no one would deny that *Ulysses*, on which his reputation largely rests, changed the course of literature in the twentieth century. His work casts a long shadow and some writers have tended to see him as the bane of their literary existence. More recently, Roddy Doyle argued that novelists today, particularly Irish ones, can hardly write a line without everyone suspecting that Joyce did it first. His remarks triggered a heated debate about the academic industry that, with few exceptions, unself-consciously supports him. Negative assessments of Joyce have occasionally popped up over the years, but they have been few and far between. Some dismissed Doyle's comments or attributed them to pangs of jealousy, but he did make a few valid points: even its most ardent supporters would admit that *Ulysses* would have benefited from a good editor, and it is true that people who praise the novel publicly often remain unmoved by it in private. I cannot imagine that there will be a day when people stop reading Joyce, but I think it is refreshing intermittently to ask why we read him. Considering the contemporary praise and his secure place in literary history, it is hard to believe that Joyce's books were banned in Ireland until the 1960s, and his name was, for a long time, a bad word not to be uttered in many Irish households.

In the previous chapter I briefly discussed how formative the Triestine decade was to Joyce's intellectual and artistic growth. In these years when he was forging ahead with his fiction, you will remember, he was occasionally employed as a journalist, translator, and lecturer. The so-called Triestine writings, which were published posthumously in 1959, enable us to better understand just how he was developing as a writer during these years. In addition, they provide more candid reflections than in his fiction about his relationship with Ireland and the Irish and his various attempts to come to terms with his role as the exiled Irishman, who wrote in English and spent his adult life in Europe. Although far away in Trieste, Joyce thought that he was still helping Ireland in her hour of need, particularly with his articles in *Il Piccolo della Sera*. In the heated exchange in 1912 between Joyce and George Roberts over *Dubliners*, he used them as irrefutable evidence of his patriotism and made the claim that "he was probably the only Irishman who wrote leading articles for the Italian press and that all his articles in 'Il Piccolo' were about Ireland and the Irish people" (*LII*, 316). There is no better way to learn about Joyce and Ireland than to look at these particularly rich examples of the Irish Joyce writing in Italian *on* Ireland.

Joyce the journalist

Joyce was born and raised in nineteenth-century Ireland, but he matured in twentieth-century Europe. The Ireland Joyce knew from his first twenty-two years was an underdeveloped and unindustrialized British colony and had been for centuries. There were a number of key events in the nineteenth century that shaped the intellectual, social, and political climate he grew up in. Under the 1800 Act of Union, Ireland was officially established as a British colony. The 1840s saw the rise of the "Young Ireland" movement made up of Irish intellectuals, who wanted an independent, Irish-speaking Ireland. The radical wing of this group led a rebellion in 1848 but it was definitively quelled. It was also during the 1840s that the potato famine arrived in Ireland. The deaths caused by the famine, combined with mass emigration to North America and Britain, cut Ireland's population by a third. In the last few decades of the nineteenth century, various nationalist groups set out to recover the Irish language and culture that had been lost. Their efforts were supported by the philological, archeological, and topographical work that had been done by the previous generation. Movements such as the Irish Literary Revival sought to establish a distinctly Irish literature written in an Irish language. George Russell, Yeats, Lady Gregory, and J. M. Synge were the more prominent supporters. They drew on the Irish folk tradition for their material and founded the Irish Literary Theater (later called the Abbey Theater in 1904) to stage their plays in Dublin.

By the time Joyce was twenty-two years old, he believed that Ireland was a dead end and its history a nightmare from which, as Stephen Dedalus puts it so dramatically, he was "trying to awaken." He refused to join any of the nationalist groups or enroll in Irish language classes (quitting after one class), and took it upon himself, more than once, to openly insult those involved in the Irish Literary Revival for their "parochial" fascination with folklore and fairies. Yet despite his independence, Joyce was also fascinated with Irish questions. When he was living in Trieste, he had his aunt send him copies of the leading nationalist newspapers, and in his letters to Stanislaus (before Stanislaus joined his brother in Trieste), he provided passionate responses to the various nationalist debates going on back home. He was particularly fond of Arthur Griffith's Sinn Féin movement, which advocated a more peaceful program of Irish economic and political autonomy. In 1906, during his brief stay in Rome, he even made an uncharacteristic, though qualified, pledge of support: "For either *Sinn Fein* or Imperialism will conquer the present Ireland. If the Irish programme did not insist on the Irish language I suppose I could call myself a nationalist. As it is, I am content to recognize myself an exile: and, prophetically, a repudiated one" (*LII*, 187).

While Joyce, the "repudiated" exile, was following events back home, he was also making his own modest contribution in Trieste. Between the ages of twenty-five and thirty, Joyce, as Giorgio Melchiori notes, was an Italian writer. Aside from *Chamber Music*, he was unpublished in the English language, and so his only public pronouncements were made in his acquired Italian tongue. From 1907 to 1912 he wrote nine newspaper articles for *Il Piccolo della Sera*, translated Synge's *Riders to the Sea* and Yeats's *The Countess Cathleen*, and delivered lectures on Ireland, James Clarence Mangan, William Blake, and Daniel Defoe.

As a journalist writing about Irish politics, history, culture, and literature, Joyce was witty, impassioned, and tended to sensationalize for dramatic effect. Trieste gave him a necessary geographical distance from Ireland, one that freed him from the straitjacket of history, but the Italian gave him a linguistic distance with which he could engage more closely with political issues. His Italian articles are about Irish politics, but they also reflect Joyce's efforts at cultural, linguistic, and historical translation. What Stanislaus said about Joyce's "Ireland" lecture could be said about the Triestine writings as a whole: he was "introducing a practically unknown country."[10] He repeatedly looks at Irish nationalism, supporting such political objectives as Home Rule, while at the same time keeping a cautious and skeptical eye on what he saw as the Irish proclivity for betraying its leaders.

He was regularly annoyed by the misrepresentations of Ireland in the British and European press and believed that his occasional newspaper articles were modest attempts to correct it. His debut in *Il Piccolo della Sera* in 1907 was occasioned by the death of John O'Leary, one of the leading figures in the nineteenth-century Irish independence movement known as Fenianism. After seeing O'Leary's name misspelled in the newspaper (the "O" was omitted), Joyce complained to Roberto Prezioso, the editor, that it was indicative of the more widespread European ignorance about Ireland. In response, Prezioso commissioned him to write an article on Fenianism. Hired by Prezioso in 1907 to correct Joyce's articles, Silvio Benco recalled that there was "very little to change" and described Joyce's Italian as "a bit hard and cautious" but lacking in "neither precision nor expressiveness."[11]

As with the subsequent articles, Joyce latches onto a contemporary event to explore Irish nationalism and the history of British colonialism. In this particular instance, O'Leary's death allows him to survey the rise of anticolonial movements in Ireland from the mid-nineteenth-century Fenians to Arthur Griffith's Sinn Féin party. He particularly admires the practical, economic focus of Griffith's nationalism: "They practise boycotts against English goods; they refuse to become soldiers or to take the oath of loyalty to the English crown; they are trying to develop industries throughout the world" (*CW*, 191). Joyce's "Fenianism" article also showcases his occasional willingness to bend the facts. After years of exile in Paris, O'Leary returned to Dublin in 1885 to great acclaim and was actively involved in the Irish Literary Revival in the 1890s. Eager to emphasize the Irish betrayal of its heroes, however, Joyce describes O'Leary as a man whose "plots had gone up in smoke, his friends had died, and in his own native land, very few knew who he was and what he had done" (*CW*, 192). He would repeat the formula of the betrayed Irishman in his 1909 article on Oscar Wilde and his 1912 article on Charles Stewart Parnell.

His first article was such a success that Joyce was asked to deliver a series of lectures on Ireland. After discovering that there was only enough money for one, Joyce decided to go ahead with "Ireland: Island of Saints and Sages." It was a lecture, he told Stanislaus, that he would never give in English. He praises Ireland as an ancient and heroic civilization with a glorious past. He denounces the British for colonizing his country but refuses to place all the blame on them. Instead, he blames the Irish for letting themselves be subjugated by a foreign invader. As hopeful as he is for an independent Ireland, he is wary of the Irish propensity for betraying its redeemers and has very little faith in a literary and cultural movement that advertises the existence of a pure Irish race and language. Skeptical that a revival would save Ireland, he told his brother in private that "no intellectual or artistic revival is possible until an economic one has already been completed because people haven't the time or stomach to think."[12]

In Joyce's second article, "Home Rule Comes of Age," he begins his examination of the history of the Irish Home Rule Bill that he will return to again in 1910 and 1912. According to Joyce, the British have logical military and economic reasons for keeping Ireland politically subservient. The Irish are to blame for their own failure to achieve independence. When he revisits this topic in 1910, he concentrates on the faithlessness of the Irish character:

> For seven centuries she has never been a faithful subject of England.
> Neither, on the other hand, has she been a faithful subject to herself. She
> has entered the British domain without forming an integral part of it.
> She has abandoned her own language almost entirely and accepted the
> language of the conqueror without being able to assimilate the culture
> or adapt herself to the mentality of which this language is the vehicle.
> She has betrayed her heroes, always in the hour of need and always
> without gaining recompense. She has hounded her spiritual creators
> into exile only to boast of them. (*CW*, 213)

This passage synthesizes many of the issues that we find an angry Stephen Dedalus raving about in *Portrait*, all of them connected in some way or another with historical examples of Irish self-betrayal.

When the Home Rule Bill was finally passed in 1912, Joyce mourned the memory of Parnell. The legendary Parnell was a political leader in the Irish parliament who consolidated nationalist parties in Ireland at the end of the nineteenth century and brought the question of Irish Home Rule to the forefront of the political agenda with the British government. But this reputation crumbled after Captain William Henry O'Shea divorced his wife, Katherine ("Kitty"), in 1890 for her adulterous ten-year affair with Parnell – one that was more or less public knowledge from the beginning. Shortly after the divorce, Parnell and Kitty were married and even more of his supporters abandoned him: he was ostracized by influential parliamentary members and condemned by the Catholic Church for his immorality. He died a year later. Instead of celebrating the possibility of an independent Ireland, Joyce recounts Parnell's fall and concludes bitterly: "They did not throw him to the English wolves; they tore him to pieces themselves" (*CW*, 228).

His third article, "Ireland at the Bar," was inspired by current events back in Ireland: the shooting of innocent people in Belfast by British troops and a series of cattle raids in England (for which the Irish were blamed). This particular article contains Joyce's most aggressive attack on British imperialism. In contrast with the previous articles, he concentrates on the damaging psychological effects of colonialism and examines "why St. George's Channel makes an abyss deeper than the ocean between Ireland and her proud dominator" (*CW*, 199). Joyce frames this article around a famous murder trial that had taken place in western Ireland twenty-five years earlier. At one emotionally charged moment, he describes the encounter between the Irish-speaking Myles Joyce (no relation), who does not know English, and his English judge. Even though there is a translator between them, Myles Joyce cannot understand or "make himself understood" (*CW*, 198). Defenseless, frustrated, and weak, he was "proven" guilty and hung.

In the tragic example of Myles Joyce, Joyce sees the repeated misrepresentation of the Irish in the British and European press: "The figure of this dumbfounded old man, a remnant of a civilization not ours, deaf and dumb before his judge, is a symbol of the Irish nation at the bar of public opinion. Like him, she is unable to appeal to the modern conscience of England and other countries" (*CW*, 198). Joyce may not have supported a language revival, but he was willing to imagine what happened to those individuals who had no choice but to speak Irish. For him, English and European journalists are the self-appointed spokesmen for his nation, and they turn their attention to the Irish question only when trouble arises. The subsequent depiction of the "Irish" as unruly, wild, and dangerous elicits popular support for the British master, who is forced to keep such an uncivilized nation in check.

In 1914 Joyce attempted to publish these articles together under a single volume to be called *Ireland at the Bar*. After rearranging them with the more political articles at the beginning and the end, he submitted his collection to Angelo Formiggini, a Genovese publisher, with the following explanation:

> This year the Irish problem has reached an acute phase, and indeed, according to the latest news, England, owing to the Home Rule question, is on the brink of civil war. The publication of a volume of Irish essays would be of interest to the Italian public. I am an Irishman (from Dublin), and though these articles have absolutely no literary value, I believe they set out the problem sincerely and objectively.[13]

Joyce's "Irish essays" were never brought to the Italian public, but, as John McCourt has observed, there is a "sense of finality about this gesture."[14] At this moment in his life, *Dubliners* was about to come out, *Portrait* was being prepared for serialization, the second and third acts of *Exiles* were underway, and the first three episodes of *Ulysses* were in progress. Joyce had a talent for journalism, but it was his fiction that mattered most. But it is also possible to speculate, as McCourt has done, that Joyce's journalism came to an end because he was beginning to feel out of touch with the contemporary political situation in Ireland. Once he gave up his public role as a journalist, Joyce's future reflections on Irish politics, particularly after the Easter uprising in 1916 and the civil war that led to the Anglo-Irish Treaty of 1921–22, did not inspire any more articles. Instead, they were absorbed into the very fabric of his fiction.

Joyce the translator, lecturer, and lover

Joyce's Italian translations of Yeats and Synge in 1909 and 1911 are further evidence that he was also interested in attracting a European audience for Irish literature. After failing to interest a publisher in Milan in a translation of Oscar Wilde's *The Picture of Dorian Gray*, he collaborated with one of his language students, Nicolò Vidacovich, on a translation of Synge's one-act play *Riders to the Sea* and Yeats's *The Countess Cathleen*. Joyce and Vidacovich were disappointed when, for various reasons, they were unable to secure the rights to bring these translations to the Italian stage.[15]

Joyce's interest in Yeats's play was evident when he refused to sign the petition against him in 1899 (even if he also called Yeats a "tiresome idiot" and claimed that he "was quite out of touch with the Irish people"), but his once-negative opinion of Synge underwent a dramatic change (*JJ*, 239). Upon reading *Riders to the Sea* in 1903 when he first met Synge in Paris, he criticized the play for not being Aristotelian enough. However, he appears to have moved beyond his initial criticism and committed parts of the play to memory, translated it into Italian, and had the English Players put on a performance when he was in Zurich, letting Nora play the lead role. He was even generous enough to call Synge a "tragic poet" in the program notes (*CW*, 250). Synge was the one Irish writer whom Joyce, still young and precocious, saw as an equal. He even deigned to admit that the two shared more than an Irish upbringing in common. According to Stanislaus

> Jim found something in Synge's mind akin to his own. The heroics and heroic poetry, that the Irish clique delight in, had no more significance for Synge than for him. "The Playboy," with its talk of cleaning people down to their breeches belt, was a study in heroics, just as "Grace" was a study in Theology, "Two Gallants" in gallantry, or "Ivy Day in the Committee Room" in politics, but he thought Synge's art more original than his own.[16]

These Italian translations indicate just how complicated Joyce's identification with Ireland could be. With Vidacovich's help, he translated two of the most important figures involved in the Irish Literary Revival. If he openly disagreed with their plans to rejuvenate Irish literature by using Irish subjects and the Irish language, he still saw himself as belonging to a literary tradition that included Yeats and Synge but also the likes of Jonathan Swift, Lawrence Sterne, Oscar Wilde, and George Moore, all Irishmen who wrote in English.

The kind of Irishman Joyce wanted to be is another story. His lectures in 1907 and 1912 provide some revealing examples of his talent for creative self-fashioning. In his newspaper articles O'Leary and Myles Joyce were negative examples of what happens to the Irishman inside Ireland, but he was also trying to articulate the plight of the Irishman who manages to leave Ireland behind. In his "Ireland" lecture he cast himself as the defiant exile, who left his native country for the sake of intellectual independence. For his second lecture on James Clarence Mangan, which he never delivered, Joyce translated and heavily revised a version that he first delivered to the Literary and Historical Society in 1902. Comparing these two versions, we can see how Joyce was using Mangan's fate as something he should avoid. As he would later do with his article on Wilde, he represents Mangan as the misunderstood and much-maligned Irishman, who wrote without a "native literary tradition." In Joyce's mind, Mangan was the national poet of Ireland, who "refused to prostitute himself to the rabble or to make himself the loudspeaker of politicians" (*CW*, 184).[17] Instead of leading Ireland to a prosperous future, Mangan became obsessed with the history of injustice in his country and gave the "hysterical nationalism" of his countrymen a "final justification" (*CW*, 186).

As with Wilde, Mangan's fellow countrymen were unable to recognize or appreciate native genius. Instead of celebrating his talent, they condemned his lack of patriotism and love of opium and alcohol. In this tragic portrait of the Irish artist, Mangan dies friendless and alone, and his memory fades into oblivion. As with Joyce's other Triestine writings, he is stretching the truth a bit here. By the end of the nineteenth century, Mangan's work was in fact particularly popular thanks, in part, to the recovery efforts of Yeats. But this slightly skewed version was necessary so that Joyce could introduce the theme of betrayal for dramatic effect.

As can be seen from all the examples so far, Joyce's Triestine writings follow a similar narrative line: the artist in question must be misunderstood or underappreciated by the general public, hounded by tyrannical censors, condemned by critics, and, most importantly, he must be Irish. Joyce's 1912 lectures, which he titled "Realism and Idealism in English Literature (Daniel Defoe – William Blake)," are exceptional precisely because they focus on English writers. As a result, they do not fit neatly into that narrative of Irish self-betrayal that he was so fond of recounting in the earlier years. When he wrote them, Joyce was even more broke than usual and he was beginning to think that *Dubliners* would never see the light of day. But instead of giving up altogether, he used the more positive examples of Defoe and Blake to imagine a possible future.

Joyce greatly admired Defoe and claimed to have read his every word. In this lecture he explains that the British Empire and the realist novel go hand in hand. Defoe was the "first English author to write without imitating or adapting foreign works, to create without literary models and to infuse into the creatures of his pen a truly national spirit, to devise for himself an artistic form which is perhaps without precedent."[18] He goes on to argue that the character Robinson Crusoe embodies this English "national spirit": "The true symbol of British conquest is Robinson Crusoe who, shipwrecked on a lonely island, with a knife and a pipe in his pocket, becomes an architect, carpenter, knife-grinder, astronomer, baker, shipwright, potter, saddler, farmer, tailor, umbrellamaker, and cleric . . . All the Anglo-Saxon soul is in Crusoe."[19]

Just when you might expect Joyce to define the prototypical British imperialist as pig-headed, unrestrained, and greedy, he compiles a list of qualities that emphasize industry and inventiveness. He even corrects the misrepresentations of the English character in the European press, concluding wryly that the images of an overgrown man with an ape's jaw or John Bull with his "vacuous and ruddy-moon shaped face" "would not have conquered an inch of land in a thousand centuries."[20] His generosity with the "Anglo-Saxon soul" derives in part from his need to describe a formidable foe. The colonization of Ireland by a country of complete dolts would add insult to injury.

But realism, as Joyce goes on to explain, does have its limits. Defoe's *Duncan Campbell,* "a spiritualistic study . . . of an interesting case of clair-voyance in Scotland," serves as an example of what happens when the realist comes into contact with a mystical place where "telepathy is in the air." Joyce describes the crucial encounter when Defoe tries to imagine an encounter with a Scottish boy visionary:

> Seated at the bedside of a boy visionary, gazing at his raised eyelids, listening to his breathing, examining the position of his head, noting his fresh complexion, Defoe is the realist in the presence of the unknown; it is the experience of the man who struggles and conquers in the presence of a dream which he fears may fool him; he is, finally, *the Anglo-Saxon in the presence of a Celt.*[21]

Unfortunately for us, Joyce fails to elaborate, and we are left wondering how Defoe's description of the boy visionary necessarily translates into the encounter between the Anglo-Saxon and the Celt. The realist, Joyce seems to be suggesting here, can never get beyond the material world, much as the English colonizer cannot get into the mind of a colonized Irish race. Joyce was particularly pleased with this lecture and sent it to a prestigious literary journal in Florence called *Il Marzocco*. Corinna del Greco Lobner suspects that the editors refused to publish it because Joyce's thinly veiled anti-British sentiments would offend British subscribers.[22]

Joyce's nationalistic spin on the origins of novelistic realism might explain why he could be a realist only up to a point. His own Irishness made him something more and less than a realist. In his lecture on Blake's idealism the following night, he explained what that something was. Idealism, for Joyce, defines the irrationalism, mysticism, and spiritualism that writers such as Blake prized over the rationalism, empiricism, and commercialism of their realist counterparts. By the end of the nineteenth century, Yeats and others had refashioned Blake as an early precursor of theosophy and the occult, and his poetry was seen as the ultimate expression of the imagination's power to transcend the material world and tap into the spiritual realm.

Because he had already used the English national type to define realism, Joyce needed to account for Blake's mysticism. If Blake was English, how could he also be an idealist? As a convenient and crafty solution, Joyce told his audience that Blake was Irish. The first ten pages from his lecture, which might have included this white lie, are missing, but *Il Piccolo della Sera* included a report the following morning: "In English literature Blake represents the most significant and truest form of idealism. He was not, however, an Anglo-Saxon. Instead he possessed all the qualities contrary to this type, and most of all his hatred of commerce. He was Irish and manifested in his art those characteristics most particular to his people."

Joyce was not the first to make Blake a Celt. The Celtic Blake had already been offered up by Yeats in the 1890s, when, on the shakiest evidence, he tried to prove that Blake's father, James Blake, had been born James O'Neill. As we have already seen, Joyce regularly adapted Yeats's literary opinions when the opportunity arose without acknowledging it. This Blake lecture was no exception. He cribbed information from Yeats's occasional essays on Blake and consulted the three-volume 1893 edition of Blake's works, which provide a mix of biography, critical commentary, and facsimile reprints of the poetry. This collection presents Blake as an occult poet whose writings – from his early sketches to his prophetic books – were united by a coherent mythical system, one that critics had been quick to dismiss throughout the nineteenth century. It was this mystical, Celtic side of Blake that interested Joyce most, and the one he used to explain the nature of Blake's rebellious and mystical character.

In these lectures Joyce justified his identification with two very different literary forms, traditions, and national sensibilities: the novelist and the poet, the realist and idealist, the Englishman and the "Irishman." Although we tend to think of Joyce's career in terms of the realist of *Dubliners* at one end and the mystic of *Finnegans Wake* at the other, it is clear that he identified with both: the realism of *Dubliners* was mystical and the mysticism of *Finnegans Wake* was another form of realism. When Amalia Popper, one of his former language students, published her Italian translation of five *Dubliners* stories in 1935, Joyce primed her with biographical information. Out of an impressive list of short-lived professions and hobbies that he pursued in Trieste, Joyce chose to highlight these lectures: "After some wanderings around the continent, he settled in Trieste, and for many years it seemed that he had abandoned all of his literary ambitions. He continued to write some stories for his *Dubliners* collection and delivered lectures in Italian on the English realist Daniel Defoe and the mystical poet of Irish origin Blake."[23] In an interesting final flourish, she adds, no doubt with Joyce's prodding, "that the two contrasting elements of Joyce's manner were noticeable from the beginning: the mystic and the realistic." But no matter how much he identified with Defoe, it was Blake, along with Ibsen, who would be included in his "spiritual biography."

Between 1911 and 1914 Joyce was also at work on *Giacomo Joyce*, an experimental and highly autobiographical prose-poem, only sixteen pages long with large blank spaces between the lines and paragraphs. In a series of disjointed fragments, it describes an imagined affair between Giacomo, Joyce's Italian double, and a younger, conspicuously nameless Triestine student. It is the one and only instance of Joyce writing about a city other than Dublin, and Triestines to this day cherish the complement. Set in the piazzas, theaters, streets, businesses, and churches in and around Trieste, *Giacomo Joyce* records the chance encounters with and passing glimpses of the mystery woman and traces the ebb and flow of Giacomo's desire. If at one moment he is transfixed by the "Long lewdly leering lips," he is also overcome by pangs of guilt: "Easy now Jamesy! Did you never walk the streets of Dublin at night sobbing another name?" (*GJ*, 6). When the seduction becomes physical, Giacomo cries out, "Soft sucking lips kiss my left armpit: a coiling kiss on myriad veins. I burn! I crumble like a burning leaf! From my right armpit a fang of flame leaps out. A starry snake has kissed me: a cold nightsnake. I am lost! – Nora! –" (*GJ*, 15). Unwilling to betray the one he loves, Giacomo admits with resignation that "Youth has an end" but realizes that the experience of this end is the stuff of art: "It will never be. You know that well. What then? Write it, damn you, write it! What else are you good for?" (*GJ*, 16).

In this ironic portrait of the artist as a middle-aged Irish-Triestino, Joyce associates the temptation of a younger "foreign" woman more broadly with his own betrayal of Ireland. *Giacomo Joyce* is an intensely personal text that documents who or what Joyce had become since he left Dublin: a divided self who spent his youth in Ireland and the first decade of his mature life as a displaced, struggling writer in an Austro-Hungarian port-town. It was perhaps because of the personal dimension that he decided not to publish *Giacomo Joyce*. Nevertheless, it is a key transitional text that marks the shift from the ironic autobiography of *Portrait* to the Irish epic *Ulysses*. The themes of adultery, seduction, and betrayal are present, and in the voice of Giacomo one can make out the shift from Stephen Dedalus to the more mature and worldly Leopold Bloom.

If Joyce became modern writing about Ireland in Trieste, he became a modernist writing about Ireland in English. These articles, translations, and lectures were written as he was outlining, writing, or revising *Dubliners, Portrait, Exiles,* and *Ulysses*. They remind us just how Irish Joyce was when he was speaking and writing in Italian, and how he occasionally managed to get back home without ever leaving Europe. In the seven years he spent writing *Ulysses* from the cities of Trieste, Zurich, and Paris, he came to realize that home was better kept within the pages of his books, anyway.

Chapter 3

Works

Dubliners

Dubliners is the most widely read of Joyce's works. It is accessible, easy to read, and deceptively straightforward. Even if Joyce had never gone on to write *A Portrait of the Artist as a Young Man*, *Ulysses*, and *Finnegans Wake*, *Dubliners* would have earned him a place in literary history as a skilled prose technician. But since we know that *Dubliners* was just one step in a career that spanned more than three productive decades, it also needs to be seen as a starting point, a place where Joyce was in his workshop discovering his powers as a writer of fiction. Although he would go on to reinvent the form of the novel, he first had to figure out how to tell a story, put a plot together, develop characters, and craft a conversation.

Dublin was the setting for virtually all his works. As early as *Dubliners* he had big plans for his native city and the desire to make it the literary capital of the twentieth century:

> I do not think that any writer has yet presented Dublin to the world. It has been a capital of Europe for thousands of years, it is supposed to be the second city of the British Empire and it is nearly three times as big as Venice. Moreover . . . the expression "Dubliner" seems to me to have some meaning and I doubt whether the same can be said for such words as "Londoner" and "Parisian" both of which have been used by writers as titles. (*LII*, 122)

Although Ireland became an independent nation in 1922 after the Anglo-Irish War, Joyce's works are restricted to the first decade of the twentieth century when it was still a colony of the British Empire, and when the Roman Catholic Church still had an enormous impact on religious, social, and political life. Joyce blamed these two forces for Dublin's backwardness and inferiority. If the Catholic Church had the souls of Dublin in its grip, then the British Empire had forced these same souls into political and economic submission. There were psychological repercussions as well. After centuries of foreign invasion, the Irish learned to oppress themselves. It was precisely this self-oppression that frustrated Joyce most, and he believed that his writing could in some modest way change the way the Irish saw themselves. Before any political or religious revolution could take place, serious self-reflection was required. At an early age and with a dozen short stories, he believed that he was just the man for the job. "I seriously believe," he told the eventual publisher of *Dubliners*, "that you will retard the course of civilisation in Ireland by preventing the Irish people from having one good look at themselves in my nicely polished looking glass" (*LI*, 63–64).

In *Dubliners*, we find a number of lower-middle-class types and a remarkable absence of upper-class or blue-collar Dubliners. There are also perverts, alcoholics, gadabouts, scammers, and good-for-nothings intent on destroying themselves or those around them. Everyone in Dublin seems to be caught up in an endless web of despair. Even when they want to escape, Joyce's Dubliners are unable to. The young woman in "Eveline" is a perfect example. Instead of choosing a new life in Buenos Aires (where many have suspected that her beau Frank will turn her into a prostitute), she stays put in Dublin: "She set her white face to him, passive, like a helpless animal" (*D*, 31, 34). In "A Little Cloud," Ignatius Gallaher has escaped to London and made it as a journalist, but he returns to Dublin as jaded as ever. Even Little Chandler gets disillusioned by Gallaher's worldliness and begins to feel like he "was patronizing Ireland by his visit" (76).

It was precisely the grittiness of Joyce's realism that made it difficult for him to land a publisher. In February 1906 he reached an agreement with a London publisher, Grant Richards, and negotiations moved along smoothly – until Joyce asked to include two more stories, "Two Gallants" and "A Little Cloud." At this point the printer objected to certain passages in "Two Gallants," "Counterparts," and "Grace" and refused to go ahead with the printing until they were revised or omitted. Infuriated by their moralistic meddling, Joyce pleaded his case: "My intention was to write a chapter of the moral history of my country and I chose Dublin for the scene because that city seemed to me the centre of paralysis" (*LII*, 134). As part of his defense, Joyce asked Richards why the printer did not object to the themes of "A Boarding House" and "An Encounter." His plan backfired. Richards wrote back immediately to tell Joyce that he personally objected to these stories and added "Ivy Day in the Committee Room" to the list. After an exchange of letters that lasted more than two years, Joyce withdrew his manuscript and he spent the next eight years looking for another publisher.

In September 1909 he signed another contract, this time with a Dublin publisher, George Roberts from Maunsel and Company. History, however, repeated itself. Like Richards, Roberts objected to offensive and potentially libelous passages, particularly the use of the word "bloody" and a reference to Edward VII. In 1912, after a series of frustrating postponements, Roberts refused to go ahead with the publication until they were omitted. As negotiations collapsed, Roberts claimed that *Dubliners* was anti-Irish. He continued to request changes and even asked Joyce to remove the Dublin place names in order to avoid lawsuits from local businesses. Negotiations stopped there. By a ruse, Joyce walked away with a complete set of proofs, hoping to publish *Dubliners* with his own money back in Trieste. To get back at Roberts, he drafted a satirical broadside called "Gas from a Burner" and had it distributed in Dublin.

In 1913 Grant Richards agreed to reconsider. Almost a decade after writing it, *Dubliners* was published as Joyce originally intended on June 15, 1914 on the condition that he bought 120 copies and received no royalties until 500 copies had been sold. It hardly created the controversy that Richards or Joyce had imagined. Favorable notices appeared in many of the leading literary magazines and journals, and no one cared to really mention the "offensive passages." Realizing that his book had produced more of a whimper than a bang, Joyce sheepishly acknowledged to Richards, "I regret to see that my book has turned out *un fiasco solenne . . .*" (*LII*, 368).

As difficult as it was for Joyce to get *Dubliners* in print, it was also a testament to his amazing resilience. He would often trumpet the fact that he managed to succeed even when it seemed as if the entire world was out to get him. When he first tried to entice Carlo Linati to translate *Exiles* into Italian, he introduced himself as an international man of mystery surrounded by all kinds of cabalistic plots:

> The story of my books is very strange. I had to fight 10 years in order to publish *Dubliners*. The whole edition of 1000 copies was burnt by arson in Dublin: some said it was the work of the priests, some of my enemies, some of the Viceroy or of his wife the Countess of Aberdeen. It is in short a mystery.[1]

This "curious history," as Joyce called it, behind the publication of *Dubliners* reveals just how determined he was to keep his stories exactly as he wrote them. Every word had its proper place and could not be moved or removed without affecting the overall "style": "I have written it [*Dubliners*] for the most part in a style of scrupulous meanness and with the conviction that he is a very bold man who dares to alter in the presentment, still more to deform, whatever he has seen and heard. I cannot do more than this. I cannot alter what I have written" (*LII*, 134).

Joyce wrote the fifteen stories that make up *Dubliners* between 1904 and 1907.[2] He organized them around the themes of childhood ("The Sisters," "An Encounter," "Araby"), adolescence ("Eveline," "After the Race," "Two Gallants," "The Boarding-House"), maturity ("A Little Cloud," "Counter-parts," "Clay," "A Painful Case"), and public life ("Ivy Day in the Committee Room," "A Mother," "Grace"). "The Dead," written in 1907, was a late addition and long enough to be a novella. It recapitulates and synthesizes themes and motifs from these original four categories but functions more as an epilogue. With its broad scope and complexity, "The Dead" also anticipates Joyce's move away from the short story and toward the novel.

Joyce did not conceive of *Dubliners* as a unified collection of short stories from the start. In fact, he wrote "The Sisters," the very first story, in July 1904 after George Russell asked him to conjure up something "simple, rural?" for the *Irish Homestead* (*LII*, 43). Although Joyce would later deride his early experience writing for a "pig's paper" (this is Stephen's phrase in *Ulysses*), he used this opportunity to begin exploring the paralysis of Dublin life. In the process, he ignored Russell's simple request to avoid "shock[ing]" readers and wrote his first story about a nameless little boy's relationship with an aged and dying priest. The relationship between the two leaves a lot to be explained, as does the priest's strange behavior, which we learn about from his sisters once he has died. Did he break the chalice or was it the altar boy? What is he laughing about in the confession-box? When one publisher suspected that there was something else going on in "The Sisters," he asked Joyce pointedly if there was sodomy in the story and whether or not the priest was suspended *only* for breaking the chalice (*LII*, 305–06). Joyce followed up his debut in the *Irish Homestead* with "Eveline" (September 1904) and "After the Race" (December 1904). Russell received so many letters of complaint that he finally asked Joyce to stop submitting his stories.

Every story in *Dubliners* contains some kind of ambiguity or absence that makes it difficult for us to figure out exactly what is happening. Take the opening lines of the version of "The Sisters" that Joyce first published in the *Irish Homestead*:

> Three nights in succession I had found myself in Great-Britain Street at the hour, as if by Providence. Three nights also I had raised my eyes to that lighted square of window and speculated. I seemed to understand

that it would occur at night. But in spite of the Providence that had led my feet, and in spite of the reverent curiosity of my eyes, I had discovered nothing. Each night the square was lighted in the same way, faintly and evenly. It was not the light of candles, so far as I could see. Therefore, it had not yet occurred.[3]

Coming to this story for the first time, readers then and now will ask themselves *what* "had not yet occurred"? What is the little boy looking for up in "that lighted square of window"? From "The Sisters" onward, we are in a predicament not unlike the little boy: we come across situations, conversations, and events that we cannot easily understand.

Before submitting the original twelve stories of *Dubliners* to Grant Richards, Joyce went back to revise "The Sisters," doubling it in length and increasing its complexity. It was now intended to introduce the entire collection. In the revised opening line, Joyce added a literary allusion and a deliberately open-ended word: "There was no hope for him this time: it was the third stroke" (*D*, 1). The "no hope," if you have been reading your Dante, alludes to the inscription on the gates of Hell in the *Inferno*: "Abandon every hope, who enter here." Following the colon, the phrase "third stroke" can refer either to the chiming of a clock, since he mentions "time" in the preceding clause, or a heart attack. On a first reading, both meanings seem equally plausible since the little boy, we find out immediately after, is anxiously waiting to find out whether or not the priest is dead. This one line anticipates the allusive method that Joyce would use in all his subsequent works. By alluding to another author, something he will do even more boldly by using the title *Ulysses*, he is not only placing himself within a literary tradition, he is also rewriting it.

In this revised opening Joyce provides three keywords that help us to interpret what follows: "Every night as I gazed up at the window I said softly to myself the word *paralysis*. It had always sounded strangely in my ears, like the word *gnomon* in the Euclid and the word *simony* in the Catechism. But now it sounded to me like the name of some maleficent and sinful being" (*D*, 1). "Paralysis," "gnomon," and "simony" are heavily weighted words whose relevance extends well beyond any single story. "Paralysis" is the inability of physical movement, but it is also a spiritual, social, cultural, political, and historical malaise. "Simony" is the selling of material goods for spiritual benefit, but it is also the vulgarization of religion, romance, and the intellect. "Gnomon" is the stylus of a sundial that marks off time with shade and the remainder of a parallelogram after a similar parallelogram containing one of its corners has been removed, but it can also be streched to refer to the missing detail of a story (of which I will say more).

One can readily find motifs of "paralysis" in each of these stories: for example, the priest in "The Sisters" is literally paralyzed by a stroke, Eveline Hill in "Eveline" is a "creature" paralyzed by the fear of leaving home, Little Chandler in "A Little Cloud" is paralyzed by responsibilities of adulthood, Farrington in "Counterparts" is paralyzed by alcoholism, and Mr. Tierney's crew in "Ivy Day in the Committee Room" is paralyzed by a nostalgia for the good old days when their "Chief" Parnell was still alive. A similar pattern can be found with the term "simony": the little boy in "Araby" confuses romance and commerce, Mrs. Mooney in "The Boarding-House" traps Mr. Doran into marrying the daughter she has dangled like a piece of bait, Corley in "Two Gallants" feigns a love interest for a gold coin, and Mrs. Kearney in "A Mother" ruins her daughter's music career (at least in Dublin) by demanding the payment before the performance.

"Gnomons" can be found all over *Dubliners*: they are the missing bits of information or gaps in the plot that make it impossible for us to arrive at stable interpretations.[4] They challenge us to fill in the gaps, but we have to be content with readings that invite speculation and resist definite conclusions. Not only are we unsure what really "went wrong" with Father Flynn in "The Sisters," we never know, for instance, what the "queer old josser" does in "An Encounter" (urinate? masturbate? expose himself?), how and from whom Corley gets the coin in "Two Gallants," what Mrs. Mooney says to Mr. Doran before calling Polly to the room in "The Boarding House," or what poor Maria touches in "Clay." "Gnomons" like these can be found in all Joyce's later works as well. Does Bertha fool around with Robert in *Exiles*? What does Stephen actually say when he refuses the calling of the priesthood in *Portrait*? Does Bloom ask Molly for breakfast in bed between the "Ithaca" and "Penelope" episodes of *Ulysses*? Where does Stephen plan on spending the night at the novel's end? What did HCE do in Phoenix Park in *Finnegans Wake*?

In addition to gaps in the plot, we find ellipses in conversations. Joyce often drops us in the middle of a conversation and leaves us to piece things together ourselves. When the nameless boy comes into the kitchen in "The Sisters," he listens to the suspicious ramblings of his neighbor, Old Cotter: "No, I wouldn't say he was exactly ... but there was something queer ... there was something uncanny about him. I'll tell you my opinion ..." (*D*, 1). Old Cotter stops there. Father Flynn was *exactly* what? What was "queer" or "uncanny" about him? Old Cotter fails to elaborate, but the ellipses between his unfinished sentences are one way for him to talk to the parents without letting the little boy (and us) in on it. When he resumes later on in the story, Old Cotter argues that children in general should not hang around adults:

"When children see things like that, you know, it has an effect . . ." (*D*, 3). Just as we never find out what that uncanny "something" might be, so, too, do we never find out to what "things like that" refers.

Immediately following this second ellipsis is a dream sequence of what the little boy *might have seen*:

> In the dark of my room I imagined that I saw again the heavy grey face of the paralytic. I drew the blankets over my head and tried to think of Christmas. But the grey face still followed me. It murmured; and I understood that it desired to confess something . . . It began to confess to me in a murmuring voice and I wondered why it smiled continually and why the lips were so moist with spittle. (*D*, 3)

Because the troubling image of a priest with moist lips and a murmuring mouth is presented as a dream sequence, it is impossible to know whether Father Flynn really tried to "confess something" or not. The little boy might be dreaming about an event that took place in the past or the unfinished sentences of Old Cotter that day could have been fodder enough to trigger his imagination. In either case, readers will never know exactly what went wrong with Father Flynn and why little boys should not hang around with the likes of him.

But even when we seem to have all the information, these stories still resist closure. In "Araby," for instance, the events leading up to the little boy's visit to the Araby bazaar are easy enough to follow: he has a crush on "Mangan's sister" and since she is unable to go, he promises to bring her back "something" (*D*, 24). When he finally arrives at the bazaar, late because his uncle forgot to give him money, he comes across a group of British merchants hocking their wares and flirting with each other. He feigns interest in the wares but walks away disappointed. As the lights in the tent, the little boy has a self-realization: "Gazing up into the darkness I saw myself as a creature driven and derided by vanity; and my eyes burned with anguish and anger" (*D*, 28). What is the little boy so anguished and angry about? Is it that his plan to bring something special back to Mangan's sister has been foiled? Does he believe, in watching the adults' flirting, that he has imagined the sincere interest of Mangan's sister where none existed? Or does he realize that he has confused his own chivalric dreams with the real world? The possibility for multiple interpretations is precisely what lends these stories their enduring power. Joyce does not give us easy answers. Instead, he challenges us to search for them ourselves.

The interpretation of *Dubliners* is further complicated by narrative point of view. It is the narrator, after all, who sets the scene and tells us what the characters say and do. As we move from story to story, it is not always easy to identify who is speaking and what relationship the narrator has with the characters. In the three stories that comprise the "childhood" section, we have a first-person narrator, who remains nameless. It may be the same little boy for each of them, but we can never be certain. In each story a child tries to make sense of events as they happen in a grown-up world: the death of a priest, an encounter with an old pervert, and a visit to a rundown bazaar. The narrator, we presume from the sophistication of the language, has already had these experiences, but the stories are retold as if they have only just happened, without the wisdom of hindsight.

"An Encounter" provides an interesting example of the kinds of narrative blindspots that occur throughout *Dubliners*. In this story, a little boy and his friend, Mahoney, meet an old man on the outskirts of Dublin. He talks to them about school, girls, and books, but it is not until the old man gets up, walks away, and does "something" that the perspective of our narrator becomes problematic: Why doesn't the little boy look up when Mahoney tells him to? Does he already have some vague notion of what the "queer old josser" is up to? Why does the narrator, who is older and presumably wiser than the little boy, choose to keep it a mystery? The narrator's refusal to tell us what the little boy sees could be a matter of perspective: he might not have seen anything, so there is nothing to report. But even if he did not see what the queer old josser was doing, it is difficult to imagine that Mahoney would not tell him on the way home. For whatever reason, the older narrator, who obviously knows what the old man did, represses it.

For the other twelve stories in *Dubliners*, a third-person narrator steps in. Traditionally speaking, a third-person narrator is a detached observer, a fly on the wall who listens and watches what the characters are up to. Third-person narrators are not always omniscient, but they often have a perspective on events, conversations, and characters that it would be impossible for any single character to have. In *Dubliners*, we also find that the third-person narrator often shares a particular character's perspective and speaks in a way that a character might.

In "Clay" we have a perfect example of how this "narrative mimicry" works. In the first half or so of the story, the narrator describes Maria, an older woman, who works at the Dublin by Lamplight laundry for reformed prostitutes. That night she is planning to go to the Donnelly house for a Halloween party. Along the way she stops to pick up plumcake for the children and the parents. She never speaks directly, but the narrator tells us what she is thinking at various points: "What a nice evening they would have, all the children singing!" (*D*, 96). Who says this? Why is there an exclamation mark? We assume that this is Maria thinking about the night ahead, but it could also be the narrator imagining what Maria might be thinking. When she meets the "elderly gentleman" on the tram, we are told: "and while she was going up along the terrace, bending her tiny head under the rain, she thought how easy it was to know a gentleman even when he has a drop taken" (*D*, 99). Unlike the previous example, the "she thought" indicates that the narrator is reporting Maria's thoughts. As readers, we never believe that we have unmediated access to Maria's head, but we buy into the fact that there is a narrator who does.

So far, we assume that the third-person narrator identifies with Maria, but the narrator also has a perspective that Maria does not. When she arrives at the party and agrees to play the Halloween game, the relationship between the narrator and Maria becomes more complicated. Once the children put a blindfold on her, here is what follows:

> She moved her hand about here and there in the air and descended on one of the saucers. She felt a soft wet substance with her fingers and was surprised that nobody spoke or took off her bandage. There was a pause for a few seconds; and then a great deal of scuffling and whispering. Somebody said something about the garden, and at last Mrs Donnelly said something very cross to one of the next-door girls and told her to throw it out at once: that was no play. Maria understood that it was wrong that time and so she had to do it all over again: and this time she got the prayer-book. (*D*, 101)

Where is our narrator in this passage? At this moment we can only hear what is happening. We do not get to see what the children and the girls next door have done. Because of the "scuffling and whispering" and the "cross" words of Mrs Donnelly, we might surmise that they have played a trick on Maria. Although we might expect the narrator to show us what is happening, we are instead given the perspective from behind the blindfold.[5] Like Maria, we are left in the dark and never find out what all the commotion is about.

Another missing link can be found in the closing paragraph of "Clay." When singing "I Dreamt that I Dwelt", a song in which a kidnapped woman recalls her formerly lavish life, Maria repeats the first verse and forgets the second one entirely. The narrator, who informs us that everyone recognized her mistake, represses the missing verse like Maria. For readers who do not know the song, its relationship to the rest of the story appears inconsequential. But if one already knows or cares to track down the second verse, the meaning of her "mistake" and Joe Donnelly's subsequent emotional response ("Joe was very much moved") becomes more difficult to untangle:

> I dreamt that suitors sought my hand,
> That knights on bended knee,
> And with vows no maiden heart could withstand,
> They pledged their faith to me.
> And I dreamt that one of that noble band,
> Came forth my heart to claim,
> But I also dreamt, which charmed me most
> That you loved me all the same.   (*D*, "Appendix III," 234)

From what we know of Maria's lonely and austere life at the laundry, we can safely assume that there are no suitors on bended knee waiting for her back home.

Whatever the relationship might be between this missing stanza and Maria's unconscious fears and desires, it does come to bear on the way that we understand Joe's subsequent emotional response. From the story we know that Maria is Joe's surrogate mother ("Mama is mama but Maria is my proper mother"), and he acts as her stand-in, if not her real, brother (one can never be certain). After she omits the second verse, it is unclear whether Joe is really touched by the romantic song or whether he is struck by the contrast between the missing verse and Maria's celibate life:

> But no one tried to show her her mistake; and when she ended her song Joe was very much moved. He said that there was no time like the long ago and no music for him like poor old Balfe, whatever other people might say; and his eyes filled up so much with tears that he could not find what he was looking for and in the end he had to ask his wife to tell him where the corkscrew was. (*D*, 102)

At this moment the narrator describes the situation as the drunken Joe might. Even though Joe attributes his tears to the nostalgic song and "the long ago," we might also venture a guess that he is hiding something: he, like Maria, is repressing something that bothers him.

To unravel what this something might be, we should stop and consider that Joe has been blinded by tears in much the same way that Maria was blindfolded and duped by the little children and their "soft, wet, substance" earlier in the evening. Although we never know what Maria put her hand in, she does eventually get the prayer-book, which means, as far as the holiday game is concerned, that she will enter a convent before the year is out. Joe, on the other hand, gets the corkscrew, an object that can be read on one level as another escape to the drink or a sign that he can get what Maria cannot: a screw.

"Two Gallants" was a late addition to the original twelve stories. It was Joyce's second favorite story next to "Ivy Day in the Committee Room" and caused him the greatest deal of trouble in getting *Dubliners* published. Richards's printer found the story obscene. To defend himself, Joyce asked Richards:

> Is it the small gold coin in the former story or the code of honour which the two gallants live by which shocks him? I see nothing which should shock him in either of these things. His idea of gallantry has grown up in him (probably) during the reading of the novels of the elder Dumas and during the performance of romantic plays which presented to him cavaliers and ladies in full dress. (*LII*, 132–33)

As part of his strategy, Joyce attempted to beat the censors by claiming that the shock of his story could not be easily named. At this stage he had obviously begun to realize how effective his "gnomonic" technique could be.[6]

"Two Gallants" also provides a synthesis of and elaboration on the narrative techniques and themes that I have been discussing so far. Here we find a restricted time frame, hopeless characters, themes of paralysis and simony, symbols, and "gnomonic" conversations and situations. In many ways "Two Gallants" offers something of a late style in Joyce. We find the theme of Irish self-betrayal that occupies Stephen Dedalus in *Portrait* and the geographical precision of *Ulysses*. Lenehan and Corley are representative of the kind of Irishman that Joyce despises most of all because they actively contribute to Ireland's political and psychological submission to the British Empire. When Joyce wrote "Two Gallants," he was feeling even more frustrated than ever with his fellow countrymen and women:

> For the love of the Lord Christ change my curse-o'-God state of affairs. Give me for Christ' sake a pen and an ink-bottle and some peace of mind and then, by the crucified Jaysus, if I don't sharpen that little pen and dip it into fermented ink and write tiny little sentences about the people who betrayed me send me to hell. After all, there are many ways of betraying people. (*LII*, 110)

In "Two Gallants" we are thrown abruptly into a conversation between two men whose names are temporarily withheld ("the one" and "the other"). Lenehan's emphatic retort at the very beginning, "That takes the biscuit," fails to explain what story Corley has been telling him as they walk down Rutland Street (*D*, 44). When Corley picks up where he left off, we discover that he has been recounting his exploits with a young girl, who works in a house on Baggot Street (the street where we will find the two gallants at the end).

Although it would seem at first that Corley's encounter with the "slavey" might be the main focus of the story, the narrator instead trails Lenehan, who does little else but wander around the streets, eat a plate of peas, meditate on his lonely life, and wait for the return of his friend. When Corley finally arrives, we witness the final encounter from Lenehan's perspective, one unfortunately eclipsed by Corley's broad back:

> Corley remained standing at the edge of the path, a little distance from the front steps. Some minutes passed. Then the hall-door was opened slowly and cautiously. A woman came running down the front steps and coughed. Corley turned and went towards her. His broad figure hid hers from view for a few seconds and then she reappeared running up the steps. (*D*, 54)

Despite the fact that Corley shows Lenehan a "gold coin" as they walk away, it is not clear how he acquired it. With Corley's "broad figure" in the way, there is no direct view of the exchange, only the evidence that Corley has a gold coin in his hand when he walks away.

Where did the coin come from? Did the woman steal it from the proprietor of the house, or has she given Corley money that she has earned? Regardless of what has happened, the unnamed woman is presented as a thief or a victim and the "gallant" Corley as a swindler. What does Lenehan get out of it? We know from the story that he is an notorious leech, but it is difficult to ascertain why he is so invested in Corley's exploits. His anxiety about the whole affair would seem to suggest that he might get a share of the booty or has plans to borrow from his friend. The possibility that they are in cahoots might help to explain why the story is titled "Two Gallants" and not "A Gallant." As with the other stories, however, we can only guess (the pair will pop up again in *Ulysses* still as desperate as ever).

The "small gold coin" in Corley's hand is significant as much for its monetary as its symbolic value. As many readers at the time would have known, the "small gold coin" was a sovereign, a unit of currency in the United Kingdom worth a pound. Considering that the average salary for a domestic servant was four to eight pounds a year, this was a significant sum.[7] Although unnamed, the sovereign also signifies more indirectly the British imperial authority over Ireland. Whether or not the coin was stolen from the proprietor of the house, the implied exchange between Corley and the woman represents the complicity with which the Irish contribute to their own colonial condition.

But the coin is also a circle that many readers have seen as a symbol of Irish paralysis and self-betrayal. "Two Gallants" is a story filled with such circles. The solitary Lenehan walks in circles around Dublin if you trace his route on a map, the moon pops up as a "circle with a double halo" and a "pale disc," Lenehan's waist is rotund, and Corley's head "globular" (*P*, 46, 45) These circles are there to remind us that no one can escape from Ireland.[8] They do not give us the "open sesame" for any final interpretation but do contribute to the rich texture of each story and demonstrate the degree to which Joyce's realism was shaped by the evocative power of signs and symbols.

By the time Joyce came to write "The Dead" in the spring of 1907, he had had a change of heart about Dublin. He had been intent on wafting the "special odour of corruption" under the noses of his fellow Dubliners with his earlier stories, but after living away from Ireland for three years, he decided to end his collection on a more forgiving note (*LIII*, 123).[9] In a generous mood he wrote to Stanislaus, "Sometimes thinking of Ireland it seems to me that I have been unnecessarily harsh. I have reproduced (in *Dubliners* at least) none of the attraction of the city . . . I have not reproduced its ingenuous insularity and hospitality. The latter 'virtue' so far as I can see does not exist elsewhere in Europe" (*LII*, 166). Although *Dubliners* originally concluded with a moment of spiritual emptiness in "Grace," "The Dead" offered a glimpse of some good old-fashioned Irish hospitality.

"The Dead" deals as much with "the living and the dead" as it does with the living dead. The guests arrive at Julia Morkan's house to celebrate the annual Christmas party. Tradition is not necessarily a bad thing, but in this instance there is the feeling that these characters are merely caught up in the seasonal routine. Although they gather together to celebrate the Feast of the Epiphany, which marks the visit of the Magi to the newly born Christ, there is a conspicuous absence of any religious rituals. In fact, no one ever mentions exactly what it is they are there to celebrate. In his speech, Gabriel Conroy talks instead about Irish hospitality and camaraderie, and he lapses for a moment into more nostalgic "thoughts of the past, of youth, of changes, or absent faces" (*D*, 205). Every character, it seems, has one foot anchored firmly in the past: for the aged Aunt Julia, there is no greater tenor than Parkinson (unknown even to the pompous tenor Bartell D'Arcy), Miss Ivors has rallied behind Irish nationalist causes obsessed with recovering a lost history and language, Gretta Conroy is consumed by the memory of a dead boy, Freddy Malins cannot escape the drink, and Mr. Browne needs to find another joke ("I'm all brown," he keeps saying, for a laugh). The language of the story is heavy with allusions to death and dying. When Gretta first appears at the party after three "mortal hours" of dressing, the Morkan sisters remark, "she must be perished alive" (*D*, 176–77). When the conversation at the dinner table turns to the monks who sleep in their coffins, the narrator notes, "As the subject had grown lugubrious it was buried in a silence of the table . . ." (*D*, 202).

Gabriel represents what Joyce might have become had he stayed in Ireland. In his lecture on Ireland, which Joyce delivered in Trieste around the time he was writing "The Dead," he told his Triestine audience, "No one who has any self-respect stays in Ireland, but flees afar as though from a country that has undergone the visitation of an angered Jove" (*CW*, 171). Although Gabriel does not seem to think so, he is as trapped as his fellow Dubliners. He goes on annual cycling tours of the Continent, but they are only temporary. He claims not to get involved in politics or nationalist movements, but he writes book reviews for a pro-British newspaper, *the Daily Express*, and refuses to sign them with his full name (he prefers to use initials). In reality, he has not spent enough time reflecting on just who he is and what he has become. When Miss Ivors confronts him about his book reviews, he loses his cool and blurts out, "I'm sick of my own country, sick of it!" (190). When she asks him why, he does not respond. This entire story, however, is organized around this very question: Why is Gabriel so sick of Ireland? And if he is, why doesn't he leave?

"The Dead" is set during a single evening in which Gabriel will have to come up with an answer. We get a broad sweep of the evening's festivities, but the narrator spends most of the time concentrating on Gabriel. His social interactions are not very successful. In the course of a few hours, he accidentally offends Lily, the caretaker's daughter, by inquiring about her marriage prospects, his wife Gretta pokes fun at his affected cosmopolitan taste for galoshes, and Miss Ivors derides his lack of interest in all things Irish. These disappointments prepare him for the final blow when Gretta tells him that a seventeen-year-old consumptive boy called Michael Furey may have died for her, having visited her in the rain when he heard that she was leaving.

Gabriel is physically present at the party, but his mind is elsewhere. Because the third-person narrator tracks his thoughts so assiduously, we get an intimate look into his deepest fears, desires, and insecurities. He seems to think that he is intellectually superior to everyone else and worries that his speech is too sophisticated for those in attendance: "The indelicate clacking of the men's heels and the shuffling of their soles reminded him that their grade of culture differed from his. He would only make himself ridiculous by quoting poetry to them which they could not understand" (*D*, 179). He wants to run away, but he must content himself with imagining what it must be like outside: "Gabriel's warm trembling fingers tapped the cold pane of the window. How cool it must be outside! How pleasant it would be to walk out alone, first along the river and then through the park! . . . How much more pleasant it would be there than at the supper table!" (*D*, 192).

Gabriel's detachment is not reserved only for the guests at the party. In one revealing scene as the party is winding down, he lapses into a moment of artistic reverie when he sees "a woman" on the staircase listening to music. The woman, he will later realize, is his wife, Gretta. This scene sets the stage for what will happen at the story's close. Instead of seeing his wife at the top of the stairs, Gabriel attempts to turn her into an idealized abstraction: "He asked himself what is a woman standing on the stairs in the shadow listening to distant music, a symbol of. If he were a painter, he would paint her in that attitude . . . *Distant Music* he would call the picture if he were a painter" (*D*, 211). What Gabriel fails to realize at this moment is the fact that Gretta is not listening to distant music. She is completely enthralled by Bartell D'Arcy's rendition of the "Lass of Aughrim", a song that Michael Furey once sang to her shortly before he died.

The full effects of this distance are played out once Gretta and Gabriel arrive back at the hotel after the party. Although Gabriel has hopes of an amorous evening together, he soon realizes that Gretta is "abstracted" from him. It is here that she tells him about Michael Furey. The memory of the young boy forces Gabriel to take a good hard look at himself: "He saw himself as a ludicrous figure, acting as a pennyboy for his aunts, a nervous well-meaning sentimentalist, orating to vulgarians and idealizing his own clownish lusts, the pitiable fatuous fellow he had caught a glimpse of in the mirror" (*D*, 221). He never loved Gretta with the same intensity as the young boy, and she is no longer "the face for which Michael Furey braved death" (223). Although he is firmly anchored in the past, his thoughts turn to the future.

As Gretta falls asleep on the bed, he reflects on "his own people" and "his own country," the Irish things he has rejected. This much-celebrated final paragraph, however, does little to resolve the uncertainty of Gabriel's future: Will this sudden discovery of a lost love bring him and Gretta closer together? Or has he accepted the possibility that they will live together in middle age as pleasant, passionless companions? The symbolism of the "snow" and his acknowledgment that "the time had come for him to set out on his journey westward" are often read as Gabriel's acceptance of oblivion and forgetfulness (*D*, 225).

Such a reading of Gabriel's acquiescence to death, forgetting, and Ireland does little to explain the life-affirming note a few paragraphs earlier as he lays down next to Gretta: "Better pass boldly into that other world than fade and wither dismally with age" (*D*, 224). Gabriel learns from the memory of a dead boy that a brief passionate life can be more meaningful than a long passionless one. Such a revelation does not imply that he wants to end up buried "on the hill" next to Michael Furey, nor does it suggest that Gabriel is ready to embrace an Irish cultural revival. Instead, this lyrical final paragraph with its trance-inducing alliteration ("*soul swooned slowly . . . snow . . . universe . . . descent*") and chiastic structure ("falling faintly . . . faintly falling") reveals that Gabriel has begun to see himself not just in terms of the larger cycle of life and death but in his relationship to Ireland and its place in the wider universe. To appease Gretta, he may decide to join the tour with Miss Ivors around the west of Ireland, but it is also possible that he will board another ferry for his annual bicycle trip around the Continent. As with all Joyce's endings, we can only guess what the morning after will bring.

A Portrait of the Artist as a Young Man

When Joyce first arrived in Trieste in 1905, he was carrying along an autobiographical novel entitled *Stephen Hero*. Like *Dubliners*, it, too, had "the defect," he once joked, "of being about Ireland" (*LII*, 132). He continued to draft sections on and off for two years as he was writing stories for *Dubliners*. But when negotiations with Grant Richards over *Dubliners* finally collapsed, so did his desire to finish what he had started. He planned sixty-three chapters, but only got to twenty-five. In 1907 he threw much of the original manuscript away and began revising and refining a new book called *A Portrait of the Artist as a Young Man*.[10] In 1909 he gave the new chapters to one of his students, Ettore Schmitz, as a language exercise. Schmitz was impressed by what he read, and his kind words encouraged Joyce to forge ahead. By 1911 *Dubliners* had still not been published and Joyce threw what he had written of *Portrait* into the fire. Thanks to the timely intervention of his sister Eileen, however, the manuscript was rescued. Through the good graces of Harriet Shaw Weaver and Ezra Pound, *Portrait* was serialized in *The Egoist* between 1914 and 1915 and published as a complete book in 1916. If *Dubliners*, as Joyce once said, represents his "last look at Dublin," *Portrait* is a "picture of [his] spiritual self."[11] As the final words in *Portrait* attest, the "picture" took ten years and two countries to complete: "Dublin 1904, Trieste 1914."

The idea for what would become *A Portrait of the Artist as a Young Man* came to Joyce after he wrote an essay for the Irish periodical *Dana* in 1904.[12] Following his brother's suggestion, he called his essay "A Portrait of the Artist," adapting the title from Henry James's *Portrait of a Lady* and Oscar

Wilde's *The Picture of Dorian Gray*. For Joyce, this ironic autobiographical essay was an early attempt to synthesize his ideas about aesthetics, Ireland, religion, and the role of the artist. It was also his way of engaging with an age-old philosophical question: Is our identity fixed or in flux? Because we are always in a constant state of becoming, the portrait can capture us only at a particular moment in time. For that reason, the portrait is not so much a representation of who we are in the present as a portrait of what we were in the past and what we can become in the future:

> The features of infancy are not commonly reproduced in the adolescent portrait for, so capricious are we, that we cannot or will not conceive the past in any other than its memorial aspect. Yet the past assuredly implies a fluid succession of presents, the development of an entity of which our actual present is a phase only.[13]

At an early stage Joyce latched onto the gestation motif that he would use to talk about the birth, evolution, and flight of the artist in *Portrait*. How, he asks, does the artist find an independent voice? He recommends that it is only through isolation, "the first principle of artistic economy," that individuation becomes possible.[14] It is a gradual process in which bouts of religious fervor are followed by sexual excess and an eventual break with Church and society. Here in this essay the seeds for *Stephen Hero* and what would eventually become *Portrait* were planted. He formulated the story about a young Catholic artist, who gradually detaches himself from the religious and social institutions that threaten his artistic autonomy.

Despite Joyce's bravura, the editors at *Dana* complained that his essay was too obscure and refused to publish it. They were right: the essay is often obscure, the structure is uneven, and the prose turgid. Nevertheless, the act of writing it gave Joyce the chance to reflect on the kind of artist he wanted to become. At the age of twenty-two, he saw himself as someone who stood, as he wrote in a satirical poem, "The Holy Office," several months later, "self-doomed, unafraid/ Unfellowed, friendless, and alone" (*CW*, 152).

Emboldened by the rejection from *Dana*, he decided to expand his essay into an autobiographical novel. Almost immediately, Joyce began to compile a list of characters and sketched out the general plot with the help of Stanislaus. In these early notes many of the key scenes were already in place (the retreat and sermon episode, the journey to Cork with his father, and the Christmas dinner scene), though he originally planned to extend the plot beyond Stephen's university years and into his exile. In this earlier version the protagonist was given the surname "Hero," which was taken from an old English ballad called "Turpin Hero" about an English highwayman that begins in the first person and ends in the third person (for *Portrait* it will be the reverse).

Stephen Hero grew to a thousand pages in less than a year. The style is more direct and naturalistic than *Portrait*. Joyce came up with the five-part structure for *Portrait* only after he abandoned this initial effort. This discovery enabled him to bring Stephen's consciousness to the center of the novel and resulted in an economy of style and structural coherence that the earlier novel lacked. It was also a move away from the more descriptive style of *Dubliners* and toward a psychological impressionism that will be found in the characterization of Leopold Bloom and Stephen Dedalus in *Ulysses*.

Portrait belongs to the genre of the *Bildungsroman*, or novel of education, and the *Künstlerroman*, or novel of artistic development, which typically involve a young man or woman in search of life experience and success. Oscar Wilde's Dorian Gray, Goethe's Wilhelm Meister, Jane Austen's Elizabeth Bennet, Stendhal's Julien Sorel, Balzac's Rastignac, George Eliot's Dorothea Brooke, Charles Dickens's David Copperfield, and Flaubert's Frédéric Moreau are some of the most famous examples. As noble as their ambitions may be in the beginning, they are put under pressure by the more powerful, and oftentimes corrupt, social and political institutions of their time. In the *Bildungsroman* the protagonist finds his or her place in society but ends up disillusioned by the ways of the world. The protagonist of the *Künstlerroman*, on the other hand, forcefully rejects the commonplace life that society has to offer.

Stephen belongs a bit to both traditions: he comes up against the social, political, and religious institutions that want him to conform, and he rejects them for the artistic life. But there is also a twist. Unlike the other novels whose protagonists I just mentioned, *Portrait* was the first to articulate a distinctly Irish-Catholic experience. In addition, Joyce gave his creation a mythical dimension. Stephen's last name, Dedalus, comes from the name of the Greek artificer, Daedalus, who built a labyrinth for King Minos in Crete to imprison the evil Minotaur. The epigraph of *Portrait* is taken from Ovid's *Metamorphoses*, and it describes Daedalus's reaction after King Minos tells him that he cannot return to his native country: "Et ignotas animum dimittit in artes" ("He turned his mind to unknown arts"). In order to escape with his son Icarus, Daedalus applies his "unknown arts" and fashions wings made of wax and feathers. Icarus flies too close to the sun, his wings melt, and he plunges to his death. The myth of Daedalus and Icarus provides two possible destinies for Stephen: he can be the father artificer or the rebellious son.

Portrait follows Stephen Dedalus from childhood until about the age of twenty. As the title itself implies, the dramatic action is organized around the formative moments that lead up to Stephen's decision to become an artist and leave Ireland. The plot proceeds chronologically and each chapter identifies a significant stage in his emotional, intellectual, and artistic development. In *Dubliners* Joyce had already found a way to unite disparate stories under a single theme (paralysis), city (Dublin), and life-cycle (childhood, adolescence, maturity, and public life), and in *Stephen Hero* he learned how to develop a more extended narrative. In *Portrait* Joyce learned how to write a novel. It is an autobiography of sorts that begins with a third-person narrator and ends with a first-person narrator. Joyce adapted the form of the auto-biography, but the characters and events, though loosely based on real people and real events, are creatively refracted through the consciousness of a fictional character. Stephen Dedalus, to put it bluntly, is not James Joyce even if so many of Stephen's experiences have a biographical correlative.

As with *Dubliners*, Joyce represented the complex inner lives of his characters by experimenting with point of view. Stephen is the unifying consciousness for each of the five chapters, and we see the world as he does. When the novel opens, he is a young child listening to the stories of his father: "Once upon a time and a very good time it was there was a moocow coming down along the road and this moocow that was coming down along the road met a nicens little boy named baby tuckoo . . ." (*P*, 3). At this point Stephen cannot speak, but he can listen. He experiences the world through basic sensory impressions: sight, sound, touch, taste, and smell. Throughout Chapter 1 he learns to distinguish between pleasant and unpleasant (sometimes painful) sensations. The body will become a contentious site for Stephen. He will be forced to decide between a life in the Church that wants him to repress bodily desire and an independent artistic life in which he can embrace it.

We can chart Stephen's development throughout the novel by his capacity to rationalize the world around him. We first find him passively processing the world through his body, but he soon moves into the more complicated socialization process. The childlike simplicity of the first chapter gives way to an increasingly sophisticated style that mimics Stephen's intellectual growth. In the second, third, and fourth chapters, the language becomes more complex because his mind is developing, and he is beginning to find ways to express himself. As Stephen learns about the world, his observations are accompanied by more intense intellectual reflections.

At Clongowes Wood College when still a young boy, for instance, he thinks about big ideas like "politics" and "the universe," but he still does not know what they mean: "It pained him that he did not know well what politics meant and that he did not know where the universe ended. He felt small and weak. When would he be like the fellows in poetry and rhetoric?" (*P*, 14). As

Stephen gets older, big ideas like politics and the universe will begin to make sense to him. He might never find out where the universe ends, but he will be able to find his place in it. Early on in Chapter 2, Stephen cannot return to Clongowes Wood College because his father can no longer afford the fees: "In a vague way he understood that his father was in trouble and that this was the reason why he himself had not been sent back to Clongowes. For some time he had felt the slight changes in his house; and these changes in what he had deemed unchangeable were so many slight shocks to his boyish conception of the world" (*P*, 67). Since we see the world from Stephen's perspective, we do not get an explanation for the financial causes behind these changes in the Dedalus household. Instead, he records only how it affects his own "boyish conception of the world."

In the final pages of *Portrait*, when Stephen is a "young man," we come across an abrupt series of journal entries. The third-person narrator disappears at this point, and Stephen begins to speak (or write) in the first person. This dramatic shift indicates that Stephen has found a voice, and he is finally able to narrate his own experiences directly. The style is less dense, and Stephen even seems to have found a sense of humor. As playful as many of these journal entries are, they represent a necessary step in his development as an artist. He is no longer the passive child listening to stories. He is the adult conjuring them up from his own experiences. The gestation motif of the original "Portrait" essay, which I mentioned earlier, achieves its full resonance here. Stephen reflects on the previous twenty years of his life and understands that his future requires living with, not breaking with, the past. His entry for 6 April provides a perfect synopsis: "The past is consumed in the present and the present is living only because it brings forth the future" (*P*, 273).

Before analyzing the steps involved in Stephen's development as an artist, it helps to have a general sense of what happens in the individual chapters. In Chapter 1, Stephen is a child passively absorbing impressions from the world around him, first at home and then at Clongowes Wood College, a Jesuit boarding school for boys. During the explosive Christmas dinner scene, his Aunt "Dante" Riordan argues with his father and Mr. Casey over the death of Parnell, whose ghost haunts "Ivy Day in the Committee Room" in *Dubliners*. Although Stephen is not always conscious of it, he associates betrayal with Parnell's tragic downfall. He gets his first taste of betrayal when Father Dolan beats him unjustly at the end of Chapter 1.

In Chapter 2 the Dedalus family moves from the suburb of Blackrock to the city of Dublin. Because of his father's financial troubles, Stephen is unable to return to Clongowes Wood College and he soon begins attending a Jesuit day school, Belvedere College. It is here that he begins to discover his talents as an essay writer and actor, but he feels "that he was different from the others" (*P*, 67). He stages a mini-rebellion against his fellow classmates when he chooses Lord Byron as the "best poet." As part of the punishment, they beat him against a barbed-wire fence. When Stephen accompanies his father on a trip to Cork, he confronts his father's frailties and feels that "his childhood was dead" (*P*, 102). By the end of the chapter, Stephen can no longer repress his adolescent sexual urges, and he visits a prostitute for the first time.

In Chapter 3 he goes on a retreat with the Jesuits. After hearing a terrifying sermon about hell, damnation, and eternal punishment, Stephen is horrified and repents of his sinful ways. When the retreat is over, he confesses to a Capuchin priest and vows to live a virtuous life. In Chapter 4, he mortifies his five senses to repel physical desire. Soon his religious dedication catches the attention of the director of studies at Belvedere College, and he is asked to consider a life in the priesthood. He refuses. Shortly after his refusal, he sees a young girl wading in the water and vows to accept a life of the senses.

In Chapter 5 Stephen stages his rebellion more openly. Throughout the chapter he outlines an aesthetic theory and writes a poem (I will return to the poem at the end of this section). In a series of three conversations with Davin, Lynch, and Cranly, he explains why he must break with his nation, home, and church. Voluntary exile is the price Stephen must pay for an artistic life. But in this rejection he paradoxically embraces this same church, society, and nation precisely because he needs to write about his own life experience.

In what follows I will focus on some of the central themes and issues in the novel: betrayal, language, politics, religion, and art. While I will analyze them separately, they are, in fact, mutually constitutive. Stephen will learn over the course of his early life that language and politics are as intertwined as art and religion. Part of achieving his independence involves wresting language and art away from the religious, political, and social institutions that attempt to coopt them.

Stephen can achieve his independence only by imagining that the entire city of Dublin is out to betray him. He is obsessed with betrayal and looks at everyone around him as a potential traitor: fathers, brothers, priests, prostitutes, crushes, and friends. Most obsessions can be traced back to an early and traumatic childhood experience. For Stephen, it is the explosive Christmas dinner scene when he hears his father rage against the Catholic Church for leaving Parnell in his hour of need: "When he was down they turned on him to betray him and rend him like rats in the sewer" (*P*, 33). Stephen, as his aunt suspected, remembers these words, but he will have his own reasons for associating the Church with betrayal. Late in Chapter 1, when he breaks his glasses during recess and returns to class unable to complete his assignment, the prefect of studies, Father Dolan, accuses him of being a "lazy little schemer" (*P*, 51). To punish him, Father Dolan beats Stephen's hands with a stick. Such an unjustified beating by a Jesuit priest in front of the entire class reaffirms Stephen's sense that he has been unjustly treated. Unwilling to let the prefect off the hook, Stephen does what any proud nine-year-old might do: he asks for justice from the rector, the Reverend John Conmee, S.J. (he will later appear in the "Wandering Rocks" episode of *Ulysses*). In his encounter with Father Conmee, Stephen wins a small victory, but his distrust of priests is now firmly in place. Instead of brothers, they become potential rivals.

Stephen's experience with the priest also teaches him an early and valuable lesson about language. Words do not always mean what they say. Father Moran thinks Stephen is playing a trick on him to get out of his lesson, but Stephen has no idea what "trick" he means: "Why did he say he knew that trick?" (*P*, 51). Central to Stephen's education, artistic and otherwise, is the gradual command he takes of language. He learns to make words belong to him by personalizing the definitions. As a young boy, he thinks about how the word for "rose" can conjure up the colours of lavender, cream, and pink. This leads him to wonder if you could have a "green rose": "Perhaps a wild rose might be like those colours and he remembered the song about the wild rose blossoms on the little green place. But you could not have a green rose. But perhaps somewhere in the world you could" (*P*, 9). Without being aware of it, Stephen has, in fact, brought a "green rose" into the world precisely by naming it. When remembering the litany of the Blessed Virgin called Tower of Ivory, he thinks of ivory in terms of the "long white hands" that his neighbor Eileen once used to cover his eyes: "That was ivory: a cold white thing" (*P*, 35). The word "wine" conjures up the color "dark purple" and images of Grecian houses (*P*, 47). But when Stephen smells wine on the rector's breath, the Grecian houses and purple disappear, and he feels sick to his stomach.

There are some words that Stephen cannot understand as a child. When Stephen's classmate, Simon Moonan, is called a "suck," he does not know what to make of it: "Suck was a queer word. The fellow called Simon Moonan that name because Simon Moonan used to tie the prefect's sleeve behind his back and the prefect used to let on to be angry" (*P*, 8). Stephen is way off the mark here. "Suck" is slang for "sycophant," but Stephen mistakenly associates it with the act of tying the prefect's sleeves behind his back. As Stephen continues to unpack this term, he makes a random onomatopoeic identification. The word "suck" sounds like water running down a drain after a chain has been pulled up: "And when it had all gone down slowly the hole in the basin had made a sound like that: suck. Only louder" (*P*, 8).

A number of readers have argued that there is also a sexual meaning for "suck" that Stephen is too young to get. Not long after this incident in the schoolyard, Stephen finds out that the "suck" Simon Moonan was caught "smugging," a slang term for amorous homosexual behavior, in the square with another boy. Stephen is as confused by "smugging" as he was by "suck," but he still makes an association based on his limited life experience: "But why in the square? You went there when you wanted to do something. It was all thick slabs of slate and water trickled all day out of tiny pinholes and there was a queer smell of stale water there" (*P*, 43). Although he does not fully grasp the implied sexual content, the associations that he makes with "smugging" and "suck" are the same: water, holes, and queer. Suck is a "queer" word associated with water; "smugging" is a word that reminds him of a "queer smell." Jeri Johnson has pointed out that the word "queer" can mean eccentric, drunk, and bad, but it is almost impossible for modern readers not to think of "homosexual."

The language that the adults speak also confuses Stephen, but it has more to do with politics than the playground. Early in Chapter 2, he listens to his Uncle Charles discuss "Irish politics." Stephen does not know what Uncle Charles and his friends are on about, but he realizes that he can make foreign words familiar by committing them to memory:

> Words which he did not understand he said over and over to himself
> till he had learned them by heart: and through them he had glimpses
> of the real world about him. The hour when he too would take part in
> the life of that world seemed drawing near and in secret he began to
> make ready for the great part which he felt awaited him, the nature
> of which he only dimly apprehended. (*P*, 64)

In this vague prophecy of Stephen's future as a wordsmith, he imagines that the "word" gives him access to the "world." If he can harness and control language through memory, he will be able to shape the reality around him. At a much later phase in his linguistic development, he will come to realize that words have an independent existence for him, and through them he can contemplate "an inner world of individual emotions mirrored perfectly in a lucid supple periodic prose" (*P*, 180–81).

As an Irishman, Stephen also learns that the English language has a complicated history in Ireland. Although he repeatedly thinks that adults talk about politics, he will come to understand that the very language they speak, English or Irish, is political. During the nineteenth century, a number of nationalist groups blamed the rapid Anglicization of Ireland on centuries of British colonization. In an effort to recover a lost language and tradition, groups like the Gaelic League were founded to teach the Irish language and culture to a generation that had grown up speaking English (the majority of native Irish speakers were primarily relegated to the west of Ireland).

From his early days at Belvedere, various Irish nationalist groups attempt to enlist Stephen to their cause. At a pep rally he is told to "raise up her [Ireland's] fallen language and tradition," but he soon loses interest (*P*, 88). At this point in his life, he is uninterested in the national revival not because of its politics, but because it asks him to belong to the group. He prefers to be "far from them, beyond their call, alone or in the company of phantasmal comrades" (*P*, 89). When he is old enough to articulate his rejection of Irish nationalism more clearly, he tells his friend Davin that the Irish "threw off their language and took another . . . They allowed a handful of foreigners to subject them. Do you fancy I am going to pay in my own life and person debts they made? What for?" (*P*, 220). For Stephen, the Irish are as much players complicit in their own oppression as they are victims of a foreign power. The solutions offered by Davin and other nationalists like him will not give Stephen the independence he wants. "I shall express myself as I am," he says (*P*, 220). By aligning himself with any movement, Irish or otherwise, he would have to give up his own voice and pay for the "debts" of others.

Stephen's fierce rejection of the Irish language is fraught with contradictions. On the one hand, he believes that a language, once lost, should not be resuscitated in the present for political reasons. On the other hand, he embraces the English language knowing that it is the language imposed on Ireland by the British Empire. He will choose to speak (and eventually write in) English but he is always conscious of its history and politics in Ireland. It is a native tongue for him, something he was born into, but it is also, historically speaking, an acquired tongue in Ireland.

In one decisive encounter, the English dean of Belvedere claims never to have heard the word "tundish." When Stephen assures him that it means "funnel," the dean mistakenly assumes that it must be Irish. It is, in fact, an English word, and Stephen translates this misunderstanding into a charged symbolic victory for the colonized Irishman over the colonizing English speaker. He knows English better than his English master. Looking back on this experience in his journal, he is even more unforgiving of the dean's ignorance: "Damn the dean of studies and his funnel! What did he come here for to teach us his own language or to learn it from us? Damn him one way or another" (*P*, 274). Shortly after this exchange, Stephen reflects on the psychological effects of this linguistic divide:

> The language in which we are speaking is his before it is mine. How different are the words *home, Christ, ale, master,* on his lips and on mine! I cannot speak or write, these words without unrest of spirit. His language, so familiar and so foreign, will always be for me an acquired speech. I have not made or accepted its words. My voice holds them at bay. My soul frets in the shadow of his language. (*P*, 205)

Stephen may never feel at home in the English language, but by using it to articulate an Irish experience he can make it foreign to the English.

In addition to Irish nationalists and English deans, Stephen must confront Jesuit priests. Having observed his religious devotion after the retreat, the director of studies at Belvedere asks Stephen to consider a life in the priesthood. As tempted as Stephen is by the "secret knowledge" and "secret power," he also realizes that he will have to deny the senses and accept a "passionless life" (*P*, 172, 174). We never see Stephen refuse the vocation directly. It is another "gnomonic" instance like those we find in *Dubliners*. Instead, the third-person narrator accesses Stephen's thoughts as he walks home from the priest's office. This absence of a straight refusal demonstrates that Stephen has already begun to internalize the experience and transform it into the stuff of art. Instead of saying "No" (or more appropriately "*non serviam: I will not serve,*" 126), he stages his denial by repeating the word "fall," one that alludes simultaneously to the fall of Lucifer from heaven, the fall of Adam and Eve, and the denial of eternal life offered through the crucifixion of Jesus Christ: "The snares of the world were its ways of sin. He would fall. He had not yet fallen but he would fall silently, in an instant. Not to fall was too hard, too hard: and he felt the silent lapse of his soul, as it would be at some instant to come falling, falling but not yet fallen, still unfallen but about to fall" (*P*, 175).[15] Stephen's tortured mind is reflected in the gnarled syntax as it struggles to express a fall that has both happened (because he will not accept the priestly "vocation") and is about to happen (because he will sin many times in the future). It is only the next day that we find out for sure: "He had refused" (*P*, 179).

When asking Stephen to consider the vocation, the priest urges him to remember his patron saint, St. Stephen ("make a novena to your holy patron saint, the first martyr," 173). Once he refuses, he conjures up the image of his patron pagan, Daedelus:

> Now as never before, his strange name seemed to him a prophecy . . .
> Now, at the name of the fabulous artificer, he seemed to hear the noise of dim waves and to see a winged form flying above the waves and slowly climbing the air. What did it mean? Was it a quaint device opening a page of some medieval book of prophecies and symbols, a

hawklike man flying sunward above the sea, a prophecy of the end he had been born to serve and had been following through the mists of childhood and boyhood, a symbol of the artist forging anew in his workshop out of the sluggish matter of the earth a new soaring impalpable imperishable being? (*P,* 183)

Stephen has been waiting for this dramatic awakening all along, the moment when he can imagine himself as a Daedalian artificer, who can escape by and with the nets of language, nationality, and religion. The acceptance of his namesake marks both a final farewell to his youth and the first step in his future. He has finally risen from what he calls "the grave of boyhood" (*P,* 184). He has denied the Church, but he has accepted the fact that he will "serve" as an artist.

Stephen's revelation influences how he perceives those around him. Shortly after he imagines the "hawklike man," he walks down to the sea and spies a young girl wading in the water. She is not just any girl. Instead, she reminds him of a "seabird" (*P,* 185). This identification is significant because it demonstrates that Stephen has found a new way to process and understand the place of women in his life. Until this moment, his relationship with women has been limited to his mother, his aunt, prostitutes, Eileen, and his boyhood crush Emma (also referred to as E—C—, and "she"). He has been able to see them only as symbols of otherworldly virtue or as temptresses and betrayers.

This reductive view reflects Stephen's limited life experience. When the girl's eyes meet Stephen's, he does not feel shame, as he once would have, but guilt-free desire: "She was alone and still, gazing out to sea; and when she felt his presence and the worship of his eyes her eyes turned to him in quiet sufferance of his gaze, without shame or wantonness" (*P,* 186). This nameless "girl" is representative of a life-giving force that he is finally ready and able to accept: "Her image had passed into his soul for ever and no word had broken the holy silence of his ecstasy. Her eyes had called him and his soul had leaped at the call. To live, to err, to fall, to triumph, to recreate life out of life!" (*P,* 186). As these two passages indicate, Stephen may have renounced his faith, but he has not given up on religious language and images: we have "the worship of his eyes," the "sufferance of his gaze," the "soul," and "the holy silence of ecstasy." For Stephen, this girl is not an intercessor between his soul and heaven but between his body and his art. He has already begun to see himself as a "priest of the eternal imagination," someone who can transmute "the daily bread of experience into the radiant body of everliving life" (*P,* 240).

By the time you arrive at the end of Chapter 4, you begin to wonder where the "artist" part of the title fits in. Until this point, we have not actually seen Stephen write anything. These four chapters, however, have established the life experiences and education that he will draw on for his art. In Chapter 5, the longest chapter in the novel, Stephen's emergence as a practicing artist in private is interwoven with his renunciations of home, nation, and religion in public. He tells the Irish nationalist Davin, "When the soul of a man is born in this country there are nets flung at it to hold it back from flight. You talk to me of nationality, language, religion. I shall try to fly by those nets" (*P*, 220). Later on, he gives Cranly a slightly elaborated version of his new credo:

> I will not serve that in which I no longer believe whether it call itself
> my home, my fatherland or my church: and I will try to express
> myself in some mode of life or art as freely as I can and as wholly as
> I can, using for my defence the only arms I allow myself to use—silence,
> exile, and cunning (*P*, 269).

Stephen expounds his aesthetic theory to Lynch, who is seriously hung-over.[16] This dramatic monologue takes place as they walk around Dublin, and Stephen's more serious philosophical reflections are punctuated, thankfully, by Lynch's witty asides. Before getting to Stephen's aesthetic theory, it helps to have some background on Joyce's occasional aesthetic writings. Between 1900 and 1903, before he began writing *Dubliners* and *Portrait*, Joyce collected a notebook of "epiphanies." The "Epiphany" is a theological term for the manifestation of Christ's divinity to the Magi, and it was adapted from the Greek word for revelation.[17] Joyce's epiphanies were prose fragments, never more than a few lines, and they described a scene that Joyce had witnessed or a conversation he overheard. Instead of publishing them separately, he incorporated a number of them into *Stephen Hero* and *Portrait*.

Stephen Hero includes both an epiphany and a definition. As Stephen walks down Eccles Street (the street where Leopold and Molly Bloom live in *Ulysses*), he listens in on a conversation between a young man and woman:

> The Young Lady – (drawling discreetly) . . . O, yes . . .
> I was . . . at the . . . cha . . . pel . . .
> The Young Gentleman – (inaudibly) . . . I . . . (again inaudibly) . . . I . . .
> The Young Lady – (softly) . . . O . . . but you're . . .
> ve . . . ry . . . wick . . . ed . . .

> This triviality made him think of collecting many such moments
> together in a book of epiphanies. By an epiphany he meant a sudden

spiritual manifestation, whether in the vulgarity of speech or of gesture or in a memorable phase of the mind itself. (*SH*, 217)

This epiphany, you have probably noticed, looks a lot like the "gnomonic" conversations I discussed in the *Dubliners* section, and many critics have taken the liberty of referring to the *Dubliners* stories themselves as epiphanies. For Joyce, the epiphany represents one of his first attempts to generate a theory that would explain his art. It was more of an exercise than an aesthetic system, and he quickly came up against its formal and theoretical limits.

When Joyce revised *Stephen Hero* into *Portrait*, he cut out the theologically charged epiphany. Instead, he based Stephen's theory on a series of notebooks he kept in Paris (1902), Pola (1904), and Trieste (1907). These jottings are not very extensive but with them he was wrestling with a number of aesthetic questions raised by Aristotle and St. Thomas Aquinas.[18] In *Portrait* Stephen begins to talk about aesthetics during his encounter with the English dean. As with the word "tundish," Stephen's knowledge of philosophy becomes another way for him to flex his intellectual muscles. At one point, when Stephen discusses the metaphorical "light" offered by Aristotle and Aquinas, the dean thinks that he is talking about a literal lamp ("Epictetus also had a lamp," 202). Although Stephen mentions a few pages earlier that he would like to "forge out an esthetic philosophy," it is the dean who challenges him to get started (*P*, 194): "You are an artist, are you not, Mr. Dedalus? . . . The object of the artist is the creation of the beautiful. What the beautiful is is another question" (*P*, 200–01).

In response to the dean's sly provocation, Stephen defines "beauty" by using two lines from Aquinas, which I will return to shortly. When he gives Lynch a more expansive version of his aesthetic theory soon after this encounter, he begins with Aristotle. In his *Poetics*, Aristotle claimed that tragedy elicited two extreme emotions from its audience: pity and terror. The audience feels pity at watching someone else suffer and terror because it could happen to them. Stephen puts his own spin on Aristotle by introducing the two terms "static" (fixed) "kinetic" (moving). He argues that art can be "improper" when it has a "kinetic" effect that incites one's desire to go to or loathing to go away from something (he puts "pornographical" and "didactic" art in this category). Proper art has a "static" effect because it raises one beyond the physical world to a purely mental realm.

Stephen moves from a consideration of art's effect on the viewer to the act of aesthetic apprehension. In doing so, he returns to Aquinas and repeats one of the quotations he used earlier with the dean: "*Pulcra sunt quae visa placent*" ("We call that beautiful which pleases the sight"). At this point Stephen examines the process by which the viewer enjoys art through the senses. Aesthetic apprehension is a static process that involves the intellect and the imagination: the intellect beholds truth, the imagination beholds beauty. Beauty, however, has still not been defined. Stephen goes back to another line from Aquinas: "*ad pulcritudinem tria requiruntur, integritas, consonantia, claritas*" ("three things are needed for beauty, wholeness, harmony, and radiance") (*P*, 229). Stephen uses these three "things" to explain the phases of aesthetic apprehension that enable the viewer to contemplate the "beauty" of an aesthetic image. With *integritas* the aesthetic image achieves its oneness, with *consonantia* the aesthetic image is seen as both a sequence of parts and a whole thing, and with *claritas* the aesthetic image achieves its singularity or whatness.

At first, Stephen uses *claritas* to define the moment when the viewer apprehends the "radiance" of the aesthetic image. But as his monologue reaches one of its crescendos, he deftly turns to the artist and the creation of the aesthetic image.

> The supreme quality is felt by the artist when the esthetic image is first conceived in the imagination. The mind in that mysterious instant Shelley likened beautifully to a fading coal. The instant wherein that supreme quality of beauty, the clear radiance of the esthetic image, is apprehended luminously by the mind which has been arrested by its wholeness and fascinated by its harmony is the luminous silent stasis of esthetic pleasure, a spiritual state very like to that cardiac condition which the Italian physiologist Luigi Galvani, using a phrase almost as beautiful as Shelley's, called the enchantment of the heart. (*P*, 231)

The many strands of Stephen's aesthetic theory come together here. He synthesizes the concepts borrowed from Aquinas and moves outward to include the Romantic poet Percy Bysshe Shelley and the physiologist Luigi Galvani. In this shift from scholastic philosophy to poetry and physiology, the "mysterious instant" of aesthetic apprehension is redefined according to a metaphorical image ("the fading coal") and a visceral effect ("the enchantment of the heart"). This shift suggests that Stephen has moved away from theorizing the aesthetic to performing it, and the "silent stasis of esthetic pleasure" he mentioned in his theory is followed by "a thoughtenchanted silence" once he has finished.

In the final stage Stephen reflects on the relationship between literary form and artistic personality. There are three forms available to the artist (the lyric, epic, and dramatic), but they "are often confused" (*P*, 232). For Stephen, the dramatic form is ideal because it enables the artist to represent personal experience and simultaneously withdraw behind a curtain of impersonality.

> The personality of the artist, at first a cry or a cadence or a mood and then a fluid and lambent narrative, finally refines itself out of existence, impersonalizes itself so to speak. The esthetic image in the dramatic form is life purified in and reprojected from the human imagination. The mystery of esthetic like that of material creation is accomplished. The artist, like the God of the creation, remains within or behind or beyond or above his handiwork, invisible, refined out of existence, indifferent, paring his fingernails. (*P*, 233)

In the climax of his exposition, Stephen gives the artist a godlike role. Moving from scholastic philosophy (Aquinas) through romanticism (Shelley) to realism (unacknowledged reference to Flaubert), he has found a way to explain how the artist can build from autobiographical material and remain detached from it.[19]

After Stephen puts together an aesthetic theory, he writes a poem. Instead of immediately giving us the poem in its finished form, Joyce staggers the scene so that we watch Stephen in his workshop cobble together words and phrases before fitting them into the verses of a villanelle, a French poetic form popular at the end of the nineteenth century. Ten years earlier, he had tried to write a poem to Emma but failed. This time he has had enough education and life experience to draw on. Although we barely see Stephen interact with Emma throughout *Portrait*, it is clear that he has developed an intense crush on her. Part of his inspiration for the poem comes out of his jealousy after he sees Emma talk to Father Moran as she plays with "the pages of her Irish sees phrasebook" (*P*, 238). Stephen thinks that they were flirting, but his friends claim they were talking innocently.

It does not really matter if they were flirting or not. Stephen interprets this moment as another act of betrayal, one that conflates the two forces, religious and national, he has decided to rebel against. As much as he feels slighted on a personal level, he attempts to universalize the experience by making her a "figure of the womanhood of her country" (*P*, 239). This phrase, in fact, passes through Stephen's mind in a slightly different form after he hears Davin's story about the Irish peasant woman, who asked him to spend the night when her husband was away. As upset as he may be by thoughts of betrayal, the image of Emma and the pangs of his jealousy leave him sexually aroused:

> A glow of desire kindled again his soul and fired and fulfilled all his body. Conscious of his desire she was waking from odorous sleep, the temptress of the villanelle. Her eyes, dark and with a look of languor, were opening to his eyes. Her nakedness yielded to him, radiant, warm, odorous, and lavishlimbed, enfolded him like a shining cloud, enfolded him like water with a liquid life. (*P*, 242)

Although Stephen modeled his aesthetic theory on the procreative cycle of "artistic conception, artistic gestation and artistic reproduction," this moment is more masturbatory than anything else. Artistic creation derives from the sexual desire of a poet, who is alone in his bed. We finally get Stephen's "Villanelle of the Temptress" immediately after this description, but it is difficult to read the line "While sacrificing hands upraise/The chalice flowing to the brim" without thinking about where Stephen's own hands have been.

When we come upon Stephen's journal entries in the last section of Chapter 5, we should pause to remember the second half of the title: "as a *young* man." It was this youngness that led Frank Budgen to remark that Stephen is like "a young cat sharpening his claws on the tree of life."[20] This qualification of Stephen as a young man, or young cat, is precisely what gave Joyce the necessary ironic distance through which he could paint this semi-autobiographical portrait. It was not a portrait of the artist as a "fully-grown man." Instead, it was a portrait of one who has the potential, talent, hope, and vision to become an artist.

Although Stephen vows "to recreate life out of life," does he really have that much to show for it at the end of the novel (*P*, 186)? He has sketched an aesthetic theory borrowed from Aristotle and Aquinas, composed a villanelle, and kept a private journal. The first two exercises demonstrate that he has the potential for deep thought (philosophy and poetry), but Stephen would be the first to admit that they are more valuable as a process than as a final product. Upon rereading his villanelle, even he admits in his journal that he has found "vague words for a vague emotion" (*P*, 274). Aquinas and the villanelle will not give him the form he needs for any revolutionary mode of literary expression. Neither will the journal. But these reflections on friends, family, and Emma are a necessary step in finding a voice and their fragmentary form provides another example of the individualized voice we come to know in his more adult conversations with Davin, Lynch, and Cranly.[21] The journal represents the public exposure of a private voice, one that he has wrested forcefully from the more dominant voices of his church, nation, and home.

Emboldened by this newly acquired voice, Stephen makes some big promises. The penultimate journal entry is a case in point: "Welcome, O Life! I go to encounter for the millionth time the reality of experience and to forge in the smithy of my soul the uncreated conscience of my race" (*P*, 275–76). Hugh Kenner has noted that the verb "forge" plays on the dual meaning of "create" from scratch and "copy."[22] The question of what and where he wants to create or copy is ambiguous. A more skeptical reading of Stephen emphasizes above all that this declaration of independence is also a moment of uncertainty, hesitation, and fear. Stephen, we must remember, is not sure exactly what he is going to do once he leaves Ireland, and the novel never tells us. Even more daunting is the fact that he has brought upon himself the monumental task of "forging" nothing less than the "uncreated conscience" of an entire race.

The act of becoming symbolic of his race requires that Stephen transcend the geographical borders of his country and break down the stereotypes of his countrymen through his art. He will be Irish by leaving Ireland for Europe and by writing about his experience through Greek, Latin, and European models. Richard Rowan in *Exiles* and Gabriel Conroy in "The Dead" face a similar dilemma about their futures. Unlike his fictional fellow countrymen, Stephen seems more convinced that he might actually succeed in bringing Ireland to Europe, the world, and the universe beyond. If you read *Ulysses*, you get to find out what happens.

Exiles

Upon first reading *Exiles*, Ezra Pound commented that it was too cerebral for the stage. Each line, he thought, requires too much concentration so that the average theatergoer would be hopelessly lost between the acts. "It takes all the brains I've got to take in the thing, *reading*," he told Joyce, "And I suppose I've more intelligence than the normal theatre goer (god save us)."[23] After the play was published in London on 25 May 1918 by Grant Richards (who published *Dubliners*), Pound reviewed it, sticking with his original opinion, but adding that Joyce was too important a novelist to meddle with the "inferior" form of drama.[24] When situating it in the larger context of Joyce's work, he found that *Exiles* "was a wide-step, necessary katharsis, clearance of mind from contemporary thought."[25] Pound's frank commentary in published reviews and private letters did not dissuade Joyce from trying to get his play staged. "An unperformed play," he said, "is really a dead shoot."[26] Favorable reviews greeted its publication, but Joyce's various attempts to stage *Exiles* were stymied by critical opposition and censorship. Yeats liked *Exiles* (though he still preferred *Portrait*), but believed that it was not folky or Irish enough for the Abbey Theatre. The Stage Society of London rejected the play, finding parts of it obscene. In Munich, *Exiles* sharply divided its German reviewers. Until the first American production in 1924, *Exiles* was exiled from the English-speaking stage.

Unable to bring *Exiles* to the stage, Joyce decided to approach Carlo Linati for an Italian translation. After stumbling upon Linati's Italian translations of

John Millington Synge's *Playboy of the Western World* and Yeats's *The Countess Cathleen* in a Zurich bookshop, Joyce sent him a copy of *Portrait* complete with "press notices" (*LI*, 120). Too impatient to await a response, he immediately dispatched a second letter referring to Yeats and Synge as "two of [his] friends" and applauding Linati's decision to bring them to Italy "rather than the silly novels that the English public devours" (*LI*, 121). In Linati, Joyce found someone with a keen interest in Irish literature and a talent for translating it.[27] In addition, he had come across an Italian who translated the two Irish authors he had himself translated a decade earlier.[28] After being recruited by Joyce for the job, Linati quickly convinced him that *Exiles* would be a more suitable introduction for an Italian audience. Joyce agreed with him and hoped that their collaboration would lead to an Italian translation of *Ulysses* when he completed it. Linati would eventually translate extracts, but he refused to take on such a monumental task.

Esuli is one of Joyce's most collaborative Italian translations (he would later translate excerpts from the "Anna Livia Plurabelle" chapter of *Finnegans Wake*), and it is particularly relevant to our understanding of the English version.[29] As much as Joyce worked with Linati to get the translation right, he was also explaining how *Exiles* actually worked. Linati later recalled that Joyce, "sent me back corrections to the manuscripts that I was sending to him act by act, hand in hand we were translating the play."[30] One of the more significant corrections happened to the title itself after Joyce deferentially asked:

> Will you allow me a word? I prefer, if possible, the title *Esuli* rather than *Esiliati* for two reasons. There already exists a French play *Les Exilés* which was performed recently in Milan. And moreover, as their exile is voluntary, I think that the past participle is out of place. In English there are two ways, *Exiles* and *The Exiled*, and also in Italian, but not in French, I think, where *l'exil* is the state of being exiled and not the person. (*LI*, 138)

For Joyce, getting the title right was as much about finding an exact Italian equivalent for an English word as it was about promoting box-office sales.

As a way to introduce Joyce to an Italian readership, Linati attached a mini-biography to Act 1 in which he situated *Exiles* in the broader context of Joyce's other works: *Dubliners*, *Portrait*, and *Ulysses* (still unfinished at the time). Instead of treating the play as an anomaly or catharsis, as Pound did, he emphasized its continuity with the earlier work. Moreover, he advertised Joyce as a descendant of the literary movement founded by Yeats and Synge, "a born writer," he claimed, "both ethnic and yet without a country."[31] With his critical acuity, Linati picked up on Joyce's complicated relationship with other Irish writers: he was influenced by his country and his countrymen, and yet he stood apart from them.

Although *Exiles* was not written until 1914 (then revised until 1915 and published in 1918), Joyce had been planning to write a play as early as 1904. He tried his hand at it in 1900 with *A Brilliant Career* when he was eighteen but was unsatisfied with the final product and destroyed what he had written. His interest in drama was prompted by his early obsession with the Norwegian playwright Henrik Ibsen. *Exiles* is generally considered a minor work, an Ibsenian catharsis, but for Joyce it was not. As awkward as the play is at times, it was a formative step in his literary education, a chance to try his hand at yet another literary genre. In 1907 Stanislaus recorded his brother's boast that he had as much talent as Ibsen but no time to write. He shared with Ibsen a disdain for convention and morality. As evidenced in his early review of *When We Dead Awaken*, he valorized Ibsen's realism and his interest in "average lives" (*CW*, 63). By the time he came to write his own play, he was far enough away from Ibsen's influence but still had him as a model. Even more significant is the fact that by the time he came to write *Exiles*, he had written *Dubliners* and *Portrait* and had already begun writing *Ulysses*. His play was a detour from the novel, but it was a key transitional text through which he began to work out the dramatic action of an adultery plot that would be so central to *Ulysses*.

One shrewd reader has made the claim that "*Exiles* is *Ulysses* under psychoanalysis."[32] In writing this play, Joyce examined more closely the psychological motivations for and effects of adultery on relationships. *Exiles* was a way for Joyce to work through the love triangle and find scenarios in which it could be played out. In both works the affair (if it does happen in *Exiles*), takes place behind the scenes. Richard Rowan experiences the same kind of mental torture as Leopold Bloom in *Ulysses*. Both men are fascinated by the potential sexual encounters that their respective partners can have with other men: it simultaneously arouses and enrages them. They both have a masochistic bent, and it comes as no surprise that Joyce mentions Sacher Masoch, from whom we get the term "masochism," in the notes to *Exiles* ("Richard's Masochism needs no example"), and bases Bloom's voyeuristic hallucination in *Ulysses* on Masoch's novel *Venus in Furs* (*E*, 172). But in the love triangles Joyce was creating, he wanted the "centre of sympathy" as he called it, to shift "from the lover or fancyman to the husband or cuckold" (*E*, 165). The husband-cuckold as we see him is not a tyrant. He is a complicated blend of objective voyeur and detached participant. But sympathizing with the cuckold does not by any means suggest that he is as spotless as a lamb. Richard, like Bloom, has had his own affairs in the past. Although Richard's indiscretions are mentioned only in passing, we find Bloom involved in an epistolary affair that may or may not lead to sex.

The events and characters of *Exiles* are based on three different incidents in Joyce's life. In 1909, when Joyce was back in Dublin, his friend and adversary Vincent Cosgrave (the model for Richard's friend Robert Hand) claimed to have "walked" with Nora at the same time that Joyce was courting her. Joyce was devastated but was soon told by another friend that it was all a pack of lies intended to upset him. During another return trip in the summer of 1912, the time in which *Exiles* is set, he visited the west of Ireland with Nora for the first time. When he was there he visited the grave of Michael Bodkin, Nora's childhood boyfriend, who died of tuberculosis and served as the prototype for Michael Furey in "The Dead." For Joyce, this young boy was a symbol of lost love, and he seemed never to get over the fact that Nora once had feelings for someone else. Sometime in 1913, one of Joyce's Triestine friends, Roberto Prezioso, made a pass at Nora. Once Joyce found out, he confronted Prezioso and left him in tears. In the notes that Joyce used to prepare, comment on, and shape the play, he does not identify these incidents explicitly, but he presents Bodkin and Prezioso as models for Richard Rowan: "Garter: precious, Prezioso, Bodkin, music, palegreen, bracelet, cream sweets, lily of the valley, convent garden (Galway), sea" (*E*, 167). Following "The Dead," *Exiles* is his second attempt to examine the haunting presence of the past, and the inability to recover youth, innocence, or beauty, once they are gone.

In many ways, both Richard Rowan and Robert Hand are an imaginative projection of Joyce himself: the journalist and the author, the Irishman and the Italo-Irishman, the betrayer who leaves his country and the faithful one who stays. As with Gabriel Conroy, Richard Rowan represents the great "what if" for Joyce. Through him he explores what might have happened to him if he had returned to live in Ireland with Nora and his children. If read as a road not taken in Joyce's life, the play suggests that he never trusted his fellow countrymen and believed that they were waiting with baited breath to betray him.

Joyce called *Exiles* a series of "three cat and mouse acts" (*E*, 172). After a nine-year stint in Rome, Richard and Bertha Rowan have returned to Merrion, a suburb of Dublin, with a published book, a child named Archie, who speaks with a "foreign accent," and a marriage crisis (*E*, 31). The events of the play are compressed into a half-day or so (late afternoon to early morning), but the seeds for dramatic action were planted before they left Ireland. When the play opens, they have been back in Dublin for three months. Their return has been hastened in part by the self-serving promises of Robert and Beatrice, Robert's cousin. Together they have engineered a possible position for Richard at the university: Robert wants Bertha back in Dublin because he plans to seduce her, and Beatrice wants Richard back for his mind.

Act 1 establishes the cold intellectual rapport between Richard and Beatrice and the covert petting of Robert and Bertha. Robert plans to meet Bertha at the cottage where he and Richard once lived. Bertha tells Richard, but he refuses to forbid her going. In Act 2 Richard shows up at the cottage before Bertha arrives and confronts Robert. Her arrival hastens Richard's departure and allows for the possibility of a discreet sexual encounter. In Act 3 we find the Rowans back home without any clear indication of what transpired between Robert and Bertha the previous evening. Like Richard, the audience "will never know" the truth (*E*, 147).

Joyce sides with the cuckold though he refuses to treat him as a helpless victim. A woman's desire to cheat on her husband allows him to explore the complex dynamic of the physical, intellectual, emotional, and spiritual ties that bind two people together. Is it possible, Joyce asks, for a man and a woman to remain united if sexual betrayal has occurred? On one level, he seems to suggest that a voluntary union between two people should not be confused with ownership. If a woman goes with another man, she does so of on her own volition. Once husband and wife view one another as pieces of property, the freedom that unites them disappears. It is for this very reason that Richard refuses to forbid Bertha's transgression.

On another level, *Exiles* explores how there is something almost mystical about the love between two people. In the case of Richard and Bertha, they are bound by a "first love" whose purity and power can never be repeated. In the notes Joyce writes, "Love (understood as the desire of good for another) is in fact so unnatural a phenomenon that it can scarcely repeat itself, the soul being unable to become virgin again and not having energy enough to cast itself out again into the ocean of another's soul" (*E*, 163). Even if Bertha gives herself physically to Robert's roving hands, this magical "virginity" of her soul remains intact. But it is not until the final line of the play that she finally admits that her flirting and fooling around with Robert was a calculated attempt to bring Richard's all-too-distant love back to her: "Forget me and love me again as you did the first time. I want my lover. To meet him, to go to him, to give myself to him. You, Dick. O, my strange wild lover, come back to me again" (*E*, 162). Richard's return to Ireland is mapped onto the vexed question of his return to Bertha. Just as we will never know if she did or did not go with Robert at the end of the play, we will never know if Richard will or will not stay with her.

Central to the antagonism between Richard and Robert is the giving and taking of Bertha. Robert is the quintessential robber, and at the risk of being heavy-handed about name-puns, his surname (Hand) suggests that he is dying to get his hands all over her. In his not-so-subtle explanation of "robbers," with the subtle pun on Robert's name, Richard explains to his son Archie, "But when you give it [a thing], you have given it. No robber can take it from you. [*He bends his head and presses his son's hand against his cheek.*] It is yours then forever when you have given it. It will be yours always. That is to give" (*E*, 62). In a roundabout way, Richard believes that Bertha can never be robbed from him precisely because he has given her away already. Instances of the clasping, caressing, withdrawing, rubbing, laying, seizing, and shaking of hands appear too often in the play to be mere ornamental details. Each of these characters touch with their hands, and the touch, can be the sign of both betrayal and, at the play's close, the possibility for a spiritual reunion. Although Bertha and Robert exchange covert touches throughout the play, it is Richard's hand that she chooses to hold as the curtain falls.

Throughout *Exiles* we are left wondering exactly what Richard's problem is. He wants to be betrayed by Bertha and Robert, and yet he gets angry the moment it might actually happen. As much as he wants to be free from convention and morality, maybe he is just like everyone else? Richard lets Bertha decide if she will cheat or not, but he still refuses to allow Robert to believe that Bertha is his for the taking. His intrusion at the cottage in Act 2 reveals that he is a much more possessive and jealous lover than he lets on. He tells Robert, "I told you that I wished you not to do anything false and secret against me—against our friendship, against her; not to steal her from me, craftily, secretly, meanly—in the dark, in the night—you, Robert, my friend" (*E*, 97). What does Richard want? He seems to suggest that if the affair is to happen, it should be out in the open, something between friends. Robert's plan to go behind Richard's back threatens to ruin everything.

We know that Richard likes to hear the "ins and outs" of the affair, but there are limits to what he is willing to put up with (*E*, 115). By scheming to have Richard attend a dinner at the vice chancellor's house while he meets Bertha secretly at the cottage, Robert has crossed the line from receiving Richard's gift to taking it. He has reduced himself to "a common thief," and after such a long friendship Richard refuses to let his friend behave like a thief "at night" (*E*, 71, 85). The secret possession of Bertha's body is not love. To make this point clear, Richard pointedly asks Robert, "Have you the luminous certitude that yours is the brain in contact with which she must think and understand and that yours is the body in contact with which her body must feel?" (*E*, 88).

Through the giving and taking of Bertha, however, Richard and Robert are also finding an indirect way to get their hands on each other. In the notes Joyce asks, "The bodily possession of Bertha by Robert, repeated often, would certainly bring into almost carnal contact the two men. Do they desire this? To be united, that is carnally through the person and body of Bertha, as they cannot, without dissatisfaction and degradation – be united carnally man to man as man to woman?" (*E*, 172). Bertha's body is the mediating link that allows for a displaced union between Richard and Robert. Joyce is returning here to the earlier dilemma of homosexual desire and homoerotic love that he addressed in "A Painful Case": "Love between a man and a man is impossible because there must not be sexual intercourse and friendship between man and woman is impossible because there must be sexual intercourse" (*E*, 108).

This earlier reflection on the "impossibility" of homosexual intercourse failed to account for a third variation: love between a man and a man mediated through the body of a woman. If we consider that this affair is also about the expression of a more coded love between the two men, the emphasis of the love triangle necessarily shifts. Richard, as Joyce observed in his notes to the play, wants "to feel the thrill of adultery vicariously and to possess a bound woman Bertha through the organ of his friend" (*E*, 174). And here the emphasis should be placed on the word "organ." It refers at once to Richard's penis and a newspaper. If Richard wants to experience sexual intercourse with Bertha as if he were Robert, this vicarious act of adultery ends with the production of a newspaper article about Richard's return and reconciliation the following morning.

In her role as a mediating link between Richard and Robert, Bertha does not give herself equally to the two men. If Richard has her soul and body, Robert has, or attempts to have, her body only. Moreover, the union between Richard and Bertha has been strengthened by their son Archie. Together they have created a life, something that the more sterile affair of Robert and Bertha, if it ever happened, will not produce.[33] Joyce drives this point home in a particularly humorous way by having Richard, the jealous husband, arrive at the cottage with an umbrella, the symbolic contraceptive, before Bertha arrives. In the stage directions we find: "[*After a few moments* Robert *enters, followed by* Richard Rowan, *who is in grey tweeds but holds in one hand a dark felt hat and in the other an umbrella*]" (*E*, 80–81). When Beatrice arrives at the cottage, Robert slips out and quickly returns to pick out his own umbrella: "An umbrella! [*With a sudden gesture.*] O!" (*E*, 101).[34] Richard wants to block any procreative possibilities, but he is still keen to enjoy masochistically the possibility of a physical encounter through which he perhaps intends to reaffirm the power of his original union with Bertha. The bouts of jealousy and paranoia that consume him throughout the play suggest, though, that he prefers imagined affairs to real ones.

Throughout *Exiles* betrayal is everywhere. Everyone is caught up in the act, and the cycle is dizzying: Robert is the betrayer of Richard; Bertha is the betrayer of Beatrice; Beatrice is the betrayer of Richard, Bertha, and Robert, and Richard is a betrayer of Bertha and Ireland in her "hour of need." Richard's last name and the first name of his son, in fact, allude to the historical Archibald Hamilton Rowan, who was a legendary traitor to both Ireland and England. In Richard's case, betrayal has as much to do with Ireland as it does with Bertha. The play is equally invested in exploring the meaning of Richard's voluntary exile and return. Did he betray Ireland by leaving? Is he willing to reconcile with the country he abandoned? In the newspaper article that Robert publishes about Richard the following morning, he poses the same questions without providing any definitive answers:

> Not the least vital of the problems which confront our country is the problem of her attitude towards those of her children who, having left her in her hour of need, have been called back to her now on the eve of her longawaited victory, to her whom in loneliness and exile they have at least learned to love. In exile, we have said, but here we must distinguish. There is an economic and there is a spiritual exile. There are those who left her to seek the bread by which men live and there are others, nay, her most favoured children, who left her to seek in other lands that food of the spirit by which a nation of human beings is sustained in life. (*E*, 142)

If a "spiritual" or "economic" lack did, in fact, prompt Richard's departure, his return seems to promise that a "new Ireland" might be on the horizon, one, Robert explains earlier, that will become European. In a note for the play, Joyce suspects that Ireland is not big enough for the two of them: "Exiles – also because at the end either Robert or Richard must go into exile. Perhaps the new Ireland cannot contain both" (*E*, 172). Once Robert leaves, it is unclear how this Europeanization of Ireland will proceed and what role Richard will play in its creation. We know that he has written a book, but we are never sure exactly what he has written. The play seems to suggest that his return represents a stage in this Europeanization process. As a returned exile, he will lead by example, building a bridge between Europe and his own isolated country. *Exiles* refuses to say for sure whether this is a challenge that

Richard will be willing to accept. Before setting his eyes on Ireland or landing a comfortable university position, he must first reconcile or break with his lover at home.

Ulysses

Joyce's fascination with the wanderings of Odysseus began when he was quite young. He often thought that the seven years he spent writing *Ulysses* mirrored his hero's trek from the ruins of Troy back home to Ithaca. In 1917, with the rock of Ithaca still well out of sight, he told his friend Georges Borach:

> I was twelve years old when we dealt with the Trojan War at school. Only the *Odyssey* stuck in my memory. I want to be candid: at twelve I liked the mysticism in Ulysses. When I was writing *Dubliners*, I first wished to choose the title *Ulysses in Dublin*, but gave up the idea. In Rome, when I had finished about half of the *Portrait*, I realized the Odyssey had to be the sequel, and I began to write *Ulysses*.[35]

First conceived as a short story for *Dubliners* and then as a sequel to *Portrait*, *Ulysses* was in Joyce's head seven years before he began writing it as a novel. While Joyce would be the first to admit that his works grew increasingly complicated in scope and style, he still believed that they developed organically out of one another. *Ulysses* is a version of *Dubliners* bursting at the seams: 260,000 words with a 30,000 word vocabulary. *Dubliners*, you might say with some qualifications, is *Ulysses* stripped of the Homeric parallels: same city, historical and cultural register, with many of the same characters. By superimposing Homeric characters, plots, and geographical coordinates over the fictional lives of his Dubliners, Joyce was going ahead with his plan to "Hellenize" Ireland. The events of *Ulysses* take place on 16 June 1904 not because of any Homeric correspondence. This was the day he first walked with his future wife Nora Barnacle around Dublin, the same day that she "made [him] a man" (*LII*, 233).

Epic in scope, encyclopedic in detail, and eclectic in narrative style, *Ulysses* is famous for overwhelming, offending, sidetracking, and disheartening its readers. More than any other novel (except maybe *Finnegans Wake*), *Ulysses* asks to be reread and requires guides, compendia, maps, and a great deal of patience. As demanding as this reading process may be, Joyce believed that it was well worth it: "I don't think that the difficulties in reading it are so insurmountable. Certainly any intelligent reader can read and understand it, if he returns to the text again and again. He is setting out on an adventure with words."[36] In writing the novel he referred to each of the eighteen chapters by a Homeric title. The titles are taken from Homeric characters (Telemachus, Calypso, the Sirens, and so on) or, on two occasions, places (Hades, Ithaca). *Ulysses* is divided into eighteen episodes and organized into three main sections: the Telemachia (episodes 1–3), the Odyssey (episodes 4–15), and the Nostos (episodes 16–18).[37] These parallels were "ports of call" for Joyce, and they allowed him to organize each episode around a single idea, theme, symbol, organ of the body, and narrative technique (*LI*, 204). He removed the titles shortly before publication, but readers, including this one, still use them.

Throughout *Ulysses* Joyce weaves together hundreds of historical and cultural references, allusions, and character itineraries that no first-timer could ever keep track of: How many times does the mysterious man in the macintosh appear? When and where do Bloom and Stephen cross paths? Where did Bloom leave his house key? Who flings a coin to the one-legged soldier in "Wandering Rocks"? More often than not, reading is a process of backtracking or of

Homeric titles in Ulysses

I.
  1. Telemachus
  2. Nestor
  3. Proteus
II.
  4. Calypso
  5. Lotus Eaters
  6. Hades
  7. Aeolus
  8. Lestrygonians
  9. Scylla and Charybdis
10. Wandering Rocks
11. Sirens
12. Cyclops
13. Nausicaa
14. Oxen of the Sun
15. Circe
III.
16. Eumaeus
17. Ithaca
18. Penelope

"Sherlockholmesing" it (*U* 16: 831). It is an activity that takes readers from the beginning to the end and back again. Carl Jung, the Viennese psychoanalyst, claimed that you could read *Ulysses* backwards and forwards. When Faber and Faber planned an expurgated edition in 1932, Joyce refused. "My book has a beginning, a middle, and an end," he told them, "which would you like to cut off?"[38]

To fill up eighteen episodes and more than 700 pages (at least in the first edition), Joyce interwove his fictional storylines with real ones. This required figuring out exactly what happened around the world on 16 June 1904. For this material he went to copies of the *Evening Telegraph* and other newspapers and found that there was a horse race in Ascot, England, in which an outsider won with twenty to one odds, the continuation of the Russo-Japanese conflict, a devastating fire on the *General Slocum* steamship in New York Harbour, and the Gordon Bennett car race in Germany. While these events happen outside Ireland, in Dublin life is very much in progress, and most readers are surprised to discover that not much happens. The weather is mild, with thunder and a shower later in the evening, a handbill announces the arrival of an American evangelist, J. Alexander Dowie, Clery's is having a summer sale, sandwichmen stroll the streets advertising H.E.L.Y'S, and schools, churches, and businesses are open and ready for business. Details from these events pop up here and there as the characters go about their day. Leopold Bloom, in fact, is accidentally involved with the Ascot Gold Cup after Bantam Lyons confuses the newspaper Bloom wants to "throw away" with an inside betting tip on Throwaway, one of the horses racing later that afternoon.

In addition to compiling information about local and world news, Joyce worked with a map of Dublin in order to keep the geographical facts straight. The city of Dublin is as much a character in *Ulysses* as Stephen Dedalus, Leopold Bloom, and Molly Bloom. It has a personality as affable or sinister as the inhabitants who walk around it. Joyce had been honing his technique for representing Dublin in the late stories of *Dubliners* and in *Portrait*. It was not enough that his characters moved around a city that was *like* Dublin. He wanted Dublin to belong to him and once boasted that it could be reconstructed from the pages of *Ulysses*. He took control of Dublin by memorizing the location and name of every street, building, residence, and shop. To jog his memory he also used Ordnance Survey maps, tourist guidebooks, tips from friends and relatives, and *Thom's Dublin Directory*. In addition, he consulted the work of Victor Bérard, who mapped out the locations of Odysseus' voyage across the Mediterranean to demonstrate that the epic itself was a Semitic-Greek poem rooted in the voyages of Phoenician navigators.[39] Joyce superimposed these routes over the movements of Stephen and Bloom to emphasize themes central to his and Homer's epic: migration, exile, and homecoming.

There is no one right way to read *Ulysses*. It is enough at first simply to try to keep up with the characters without getting bogged down in the numerous allusions and references. Whether or not you feel compelled to consult the guidebooks, maps, and scholarly explanations along the way is entirely a personal choice. What follows will help you to get started for the first, second, or perhaps third time. This section sets up the basic coordinates and provides some of the information that will help you to focus your reading. Before getting to what happens in the novel, however, it helps to get a sense of the various styles and narrative techniques that Joyce developed in writing it.

In 1920, Joyce provided Carlo Linati with an elaborate schema for *Ulysses* that explained what he was up to: "My intention is not only to render the myth *sub specie temporis nostri* but also to allow each adventure (that is, every hour, every organ, every art being interconnected and interrelated in the somatic scheme of the whole) to condition and even create its own technique" (*SL*, 271). The Homeric adventures gave Joyce ideas for plot, character, and design, but they also inspired him to find ways to play around with the style and substance of each episode. The "Proteus" episode, to take one early example, is named after the Greek god that Menelaus ambushes and wrestles in order to find out how he can appease the gods and return home. Instead of sea gods, we have Stephen Dedalus walking along Sandymount Strand deep in thought. The protean quality of the episode can be found in the fluid movement of the prose and the rapid succession of his thoughts as he moves from one topic to another. For an episode like "Hades," in which Bloom and some of his fellow Dubliners go to the funeral of Paddy Dignam at Glasnevin Cemetery, the Homeric parallel is less structural than thematic. It is based on Odysseus's descent to the Underworld, where he meets the blind seer Tiresias and finds out how he can get home. "Hades" does not generate its own structure, but thoughts of death and dying weigh heavily on everyone in attendance.

As *Ulysses* continued to grow, Joyce found more structural and thematic uses for these Homeric parallels. In "Aeolus," named after the god who tries to help Odysseus by giving him wind to sail home, we have a slew of rhetorical twists and turns organized around a series of newspaper headlines. "Sirens" refers to the singers who lure sailors to their death and is structured as an operatic fugue. In "Cyclops," named after the one-eyed monster that Odysseus blinds, the lofty language mimics the epic pretensions of the Irish nationalist. "Nausicaa," recalling the young Phoenician princess who takes a shipwrecked Odysseus home to meet her father and mother, parodies the voice of women's magazines. "Oxen of the Sun," named after the sacred oxen of Helios that Odysseus's men eat when he is asleep, traces the evolution of the English language in a series of forty paragraphs, which are also meant to correspond with the forty weeks of gestation during pregnancy. "Circe," recalling the wily temptress who turns Odysseus's men into swine, presents a surreal hallucination in the form of a play. "Ithaca," named after Odysseus's native town, takes the form of a question-and-answer session or catechism. "Penelope," recalling the faithful wife of Odysseus, is one long, sleepy soliloquy from Molly Bloom. If you know the *Odyssey* well enough, you will find Homeric echoes everywhere in *Ulysses*.

In his letter to Linati, Joyce also indicated that his novel follows "the cycle of the human body" (*SL*, 271). As outlandish as this idea may at first seem, it is really quite simple. Much of *Ulysses* is organized around moments of interior narration, which I will say more about shortly. What Stephen and Bloom think about, then, is deeply influenced by how they feel. If they are tired, hungry, or horny, their thoughts reflect it. "Lestrygonians" is based on Odysseus's encounter with cannibals, and it is one of the clearest (and I think most successful) examples of this convergence of bodily organ (esophagus), hour of the day (1 p.m.), Homeric adventure (Cannibals), and narrative technique (digestion). As Bloom wanders around Dublin during lunchtime, his empty stomach takes over the direction of his thoughts. Upon entering the Burton restaurant for something to eat, he is disgusted by what he sees – men chomping on their food like a bunch of cannibals: "That fellow ramming a knifeful of cabbage down as if his life depended on it. Good stroke. Give me the fidgets to look. Safer to eat from his three hands. Tear it limb from limb. Born with a silver knife in his mouth. That's witty, I think. Or no. Silver means born rich. Born with a knife. But then the allusion is lost" (*U*, 8: 682–86). The man eating a "knifeful of cabbage" might not have bothered Bloom earlier or later in the day, but when his thoughts are filtered through a hungry body, he can see only the violence of "dirty eaters" (*U*, 8: 696).

Narration can get hungry, horny ("Nausicaa"), hallucinatory ("Circe"), drunk ("Oxen"), windy ("Aeolus"), gigantic ("Cyclops"), catechistic ("Ithaca"), sleepy ("Eumaeus"), and long-winded ("Penelope"). By the time we find Stephen and Bloom in the cabman's shelter at around one o'clock in the morning, the narrator, who has popped in and out of Bloom's and Stephen's heads over the whole day, is knackered. As a result, the chapter is filled with clichés, half-finished sentences, tired syntax, wandering thoughts, and roundabout methods of description:

The guarded glance of half solicitude half curiosity augmented by friendliness which he gave at Stephen's at present morose expression of features did not throw a flood of light, none at all in fact on the problem as to whether he had let himself be badly bamboozled to judge by two or three lowspirited remarks he let drop or the other way about saw through the affair and for some reason or other best known to himself allowed matters to more or less. (*U*, 16: 300–06)

Drop: instead of actually saying the word, the sleepy narrator asks us to supply it. Deciding not to get involved in Stephen's affairs at this point, the narrator changes the subject and lets "matters more or less."

Joyce uses four different modes of narration in *Ulysses*: traditional third-person narration, interior narration, spoken narration, and what Michael Seidel calls "fourth-estate narration."[40] Third-person narration is the narrative mode that I explored in the *Dubliners* and *Portrait* sections. It describes characters and events from a detached perspective. As a way to define them and demonstrate how they work, I will concentrate on the opening lines of "Calypso" (it will help if you open your copy of *Ulysses*): "Mr Leopold Bloom ate with relish the inner organs of beasts and fowls. He liked thick giblet soup, nutty gizzards, a stuffed roast heart, liverslices fried with crustcrumbs, fried hencods' roes. Most of all he liked grilled mutton kidneys which gave to his palate a fine tang of faintly scented urine" (*U*, 4: 1–5). The third-person narrator knows an awful lot about Bloom's strange tastes and describes him to us as an intimate friend might.

In the next paragraph, however, it gets a bit more difficult to pin down exactly who is in charge of the narration: "Kidneys were in his mind as he moved about the kitchen softly, righting her breakfast things on the humpy tray. Gelid light and air were in the kitchen but out of doors gentle summer morning everywhere. Made him feel a bit peckish. The coals were reddening" (*U*, 4: 6–10). We have three sentences in a row that describe Bloom and the world around him. But who tells us that "the coals were reddening"? The coals to what? The stove? It is an objective statement that could easily be ascribed to a third-person narrator. But since the next line places us very clearly in Bloom's head ("Another slice of bread and butter: three, four: right"), it is also possible that Bloom makes this observation as he gets breakfast ready. Since he is in his own head, he would not feel compelled to tell us what coals he is thinking about.

Here we are getting into the mode of interior narration that we will find everywhere in *Ulysses*. There is no typographical shift or symbol in the text to alert us to the fact that the character is in control of the narration. Instead, you must figure it out from the surrounding context. It becomes easier once you get used to the ways the characters think and speak. In the following paragraph the sentences alternate between third-person and interior narration: "She didn't like her plate full. Right. He turned from the tray, lifted the kettle off the hob and set it sideways on the fire. It sat there, dull and squat, its spout stuck out. Cup of tea soon. Good. Mouth dry" (*U*, 4: 11–14). This first line refers to Molly in the third person, but it is Bloom's thought, not the narrator's description. The narrator would not feel compelled to confirm his own statement with "Right." In the following sentence a third-person narrator returns to describe Bloom putting the kettle on the fire, but only for a brief visit. Almost immediately, we plop back into Bloom's head and find out that he is thirsty.

In the sentences that follow, we get an example of spoken narration and notice the 2/em dash (——) that Joyce uses instead of quotation marks to identify when someone, or in this case something, speaks. The first utterance in "Calypso" does not come from Bloom or Molly but the "pussens," their cat: "——Mkgnao!" These moments of recorded speech present exactly what the characters say and do not usually involve the filtering process that we find with interior narration. After Bloom greets the "pussens," we are presented with an interesting mix of third-person narration, interior narration, and something like sounded narration: "The cat mewed in answer and stalked again stiffly round the leg of the table, mewing. Just how she stalks over my writingtable. Prr. Scratch my head. Prr" (*U*, 4: 18–20). In the first two sentences, we notice the shift from third-person to interior narration: the cat's actions are described and give way to Bloom's memory of the cat walking across his writing table. Trying to identify the "Prr" is a bit more complicated. It could be a continuation of Bloom's memory of the cat on the table. He is thinking what he imagines the cat thinks, or says. But it can also be an interruption in what Bloom hears in the moment when the cat walks around the table. There is no 2/em dash this time, possibly because we have an indirect report of Bloom listening to the cat's purr at that moment.

You will definitely get used to these various narrative modes, especially in the earlier episodes. When you get to "Aeolus," however, you will quickly realize that there is something dramatically different: "IN THE HEART OF THE HIBERNIAN METROPOLIS" (*U*, 7: 1–2). Who put the various newspaper headlines there? Although you will find correspondences between the headlines and the short blurbs that follow, there is no single character or narrator to whom they can be attributed. In fact, the characters are completely oblivious to the fact that their actions in this episode are bracketed by headlines. This is an example of "fourth-estate narration," a term that refers to the press in France before the Revolution. Fourth-estate narration basically means that the book remembers and reflects on itself. In these moments the author is asserting his own imaginative powers and making us aware that there is someone else controlling the narration. The stylistic parodies and imaginative flourishes are supplemental and have no bearing on what is happening or what a character is thinking in the novel. It does, however, have an impact on how we read the episode. From "Aeolus" onward Joyce tries out all kinds of possibilities for fourth-estate narration. "Circe" is a particularly wonderful example. The entire episode is structured as a play, but none of the characters knows it. As readers, however, we get a disturbing glimpse into the unconscious dreams, desires, memories, and anxieties of Bloom and Stephen.

In addition to these four narrative modes, we also find moments when the third-person narrator mimics the voices of the characters and describes situations as they might. You will remember this technique of narrative mimicry from *Dubliners* and *Portrait*: the narrator speaks in the third person as you might expect the characters to speak. In *Ulysses* it gets a bit more complicated. Such is the case in "Nausikaa" where the seduction between Gerty MacDowell and Bloom takes place. From a distance, she sees a man who looks like a "foreigner," with a "pale intellectual face" (*U*, 13: 415–16). She suspects that he is in mourning and wonders if he is a married man or a widower, a Protestant or a Catholic. As Bloom and Gerty continue to exchange furtive glances, it becomes difficult to figure out who is speaking: "He was eyeing her as a snake eyes its prey. Her woman's instinct told her that she had raised the devil in him and at the thought a burning scarlet swept from throat to brow till the lovely colour of her face became a glorious rose" (*U*, 13: 517–20). At this moment we realize that the narrator identifies what Gerty might be thinking as Bloom watches her, but whose words are these? Is the narrator speaking like Gerty? It is a bit too biblical for Gerty. Is this a projection of what the horny Bloom thinks Gerty is thinking as she looks at him? It is possible that the voice has been Bloom's the entire time. He was, after all, thinking of writing an erotic story for *Tit-Bits* earlier that morning. The episode might be a fantasy, something that he wants to see as he masturbates discreetly behind a rock. Once he orgasms, there is an abrupt shift: the flowery prose disappears and we are once again thrust back into his mind. His earlier attraction to Gerty gives way to guilt, and he spends the rest of the episode thinking about Molly, Blazes Boylan, and his other sexual indiscretions in the past.

Now that we have dwelt on some of the narrative modes, we can get to what happens. The plot of *Ulysses* is pretty straightforward. Stephen Dedalus and Leopold Bloom walk around Dublin, meeting friends and avoiding family. Molly stays at home in bed waiting for the arrival of Blazes Boylan later that afternoon. Stephen, whom you might remember from *Portrait*, is back in Dublin. He was called back from Paris to see his mother before she died and is still unsure if his career will be found at home or abroad. When we find him in the first three episodes, he is living in the Martello Tower with the medical student Buck Mulligan and the Englishman Haines. He has a job teaching history at a high school but he has decided to quit. Stephen continues to pop up throughout the day, but the plot will focus a lot more on Bloom. Although Bloom works as a canvasser for advertisements, he spends a great deal of his time wandering around Dublin in order to avoid returning home. He suspects that Molly will have an affair with the jaunty Blazes Boylan later that afternoon. While we do not see much of Molly until the very last episode, we learn about her throughout the day from Bloom's thoughts and conversations. The entire novel is structured around two encounters: one between Stephen and Bloom, which we see, and the other between Boylan and Molly, which we do not.

Ulysses begins twice: first with Stephen at the Martello Tower in "Telema-chus," then again, three episodes later, in "Calypso," with Bloom getting breakfast ready. The hour for both episodes is eight o'clock, and these introductory chapters tell us just who these characters are and how their minds will work throughout the day. This shift from Stephen to Bloom is symbolic of a revolution of sorts that took place in their creator. Upon first reading "Calypso," Pound wrote to Joyce: "Bloom is a great man and you have almightily answered the critics who asked me whether having made Stephen, more or less autobiography, you could ever go on to create a second character. 'Second character is the test.' "[41] By the third episode, Joyce realized that he had outgrown the 22-year-old poet manqué. In Bloom he found a character closer to his own age and life experience: late thirties. As with Ulysses, Bloom is an "allroundman": a father, son, husband, citizen, and lover out to seek adventure in the world before returning home.

When *Ulysses* first opens, we find Buck Mulligan at the top of the Martello Tower parodying the Catholic mass. In this instance, we are not given a Catholic mass, but the profanation of one uttered by a nonbeliever. At the same time, his words parody an epic invocation, and Joyce lets us know that he has taken over the Church's and the epic literary tradition by mocking and manipulating its forms. With the abrupt and puzzling appearance of "Chry-sostomos" further down the page, we get our first glimpse of the interior narration that will dominate the rest of the book: "He peered sideways up and gave a long slow whistle of call, then paused, awhile in rapt attention, his even white teeth glistening here and there with gold points. Chrysostomos. Two strong shrill whistles answered through the calm" (*U*, 1: 24–27). Where does "Chrysostomos" come from? What does the word even mean? The narrator has simply noted that the whistling Mulligan has some capped teeth in his mouth before drawing our attention to the two whistles that can be heard in the distance. In between these two objective statements, the narrative channels Stephen's thoughts as he watches Mulligan's mouth. Instead of seeing gold caps, he is reminded of the Greek Church father St. John Chrysostomos (literally meaning "golden mouthed"), famed for his skilled oratory.

We get to know Stephen and Bloom over the course of the day and become intimately familiar with their memories, reflections, and desires. Stephen, we discover, is haunted by memories of his dead mother, and the devilish "Malachi" Mulligan does everything he can to conjure them up. When meditating on the Irish Sea, Mulligan calls it a "great sweet mother" and a "mighty mother" before telling Stephen bluntly, "The aunt thinks you killed your mother . . . That's why she won't let me have anything to do with you" (*U*, 1: 88–89). Stephen cannot stop dwelling on his refusal to kneel down at his mother's deathbed. After a year, he still wears his black mourning clothes like the distraught Hamlet, whom he admires. His final nervous collapse at the end of the day is triggered by the sudden appearance of her ghost. Stephen may have refused his mother's final request to kneel and pray for her, but the prayer continually circulates through his guilty mind. If he has flown from the nets of Church and nation, at least temporarily, he still seems to be snagged in the home net (or nest) that his mother represents.

Stephen, as you will remember from *Portrait*, is a party of one, fiercely opposed to British imperialism but deeply suspicious of Irish nationalist movements. Despite his false start in Paris, he still seems intent on rousing the intellectual conscience of his race and freeing it from the nightmare of history. He does not have anything down on paper yet, but he has devised a witty parable and a theory on Shakespeare. His style has become more severe and naturalistic since the "Villanelle of the Temptress," and during one public display in "Aeolus" he recites a playful piece called "A Pisgah Sight of Palestine, or, The Parable of the Plums". In it, two old vestal virgins, who want to see a bird's-eye view of Dublin, climb to the top of Nelson's pillar, eat plums, and spit seeds on the passers-by down below.[42] The seemingly innocent activity of old ladies eating plums and spitting seeds is reconceived in Stephen's mind as the complicity of the Irish race with their British conqueror, who is in this instance represented by Lord Nelson, a legendary admiral in the British Royal Navy during the Napoleonic Wars. Instead of national deliverance, the two old ladies represent paralysis. They cannot give Ireland a future, and the plumseeds they let fall from the top of the "one-handled adulterer" hit unfertile ground.

In his Shakespeare theory Stephen turns to the question of paternity. If the bond between a son and a mother is biological, then that between a father and a son is based on "a legal fiction." How does a son really know his own father and vice versa? Stephen is eager enough to break with his father, Simon Dedalus, but he is intent on exploring the paternal bond between an author and his characters, the creator and his creation. He tests his theory in the National Library later that afternoon ("Scylla and Charybdis") in front of Dublin's literati when he interprets Shakespeare's plays biographically. In his reading of *Hamlet*, Shakespeare is the ghost of Hamlet's father (a role he once played), Hamlet is Shakespeare's dead son Hamnet, Anne Hathaway is the adulterous queen, and his three brothers are the usurpers. Many of the biographical facts are way off the mark, but Stephen has found another way to imagine how an artist can write from his own experience. He has begun to conceive of the artist as "myriadminded" like Shakespeare or polytropic (crafty) like Ulysses. Instead of choosing between father or son, Hamlet or Hamlet's father, he can be both. "Truth," as John Englinton reminds him, "is midway. He is the ghost and the prince. He is all in all" (*U*, 9: 1018–19). Put another way by Stephen, "We walk through ourselves, meeting robbers, ghosts, giants, old men, young men, wives, widows, brothers-in-love, but always meeting ourselves" (*U*, 9: 1044–46).

Bloom serves as a refreshing counterpart to Stephen. He is less bookish, and he has the life experience that Stephen lacks. His mind is particularly sensitive to the external environment and although he is prone to serious distractions (particularly female ones), he is firmly anchored in his physical environment. Despite their differences, they represent Telemachus and Ulysses: a son looking for a father and a father looking for a son. Stephen's father is still alive and well traipsing around Dublin, while Bloom's only son, Rudy, died ten and a half years earlier (9 January 1894) when he was eleven days old. (He still has a daughter, his first child, Milly, who is now eighteen and whom he sent to Mullinger for the summer.) Bloom and Stephen cross and recross paths at various points throughout the day, but their direct encounter does not take place until they meet at Holles Street Maternity Hospital ("Oxen of the Sun") and a little later in Bella Cohen's brothel ("Circe").

Although we get some glimpses of Stephen wandering around the city, the urban experience is reserved for Bloom alone. Throughout the day his mind and body interact with the sights, sounds, and smells of Dublin. In his sociological study of the metropolis in 1903, Georg Simmel noticed that "The metropolitan type of man [...] develops an organ protecting him against the threatening currents and discrepancies of his external environment [...] He reacts with his head instead of his heart. In this an increased awareness assumes the psychic prerogative [. . .] Intellectuality is thus seen to preserve subjective life against the overwhelming power of metropolitan life."[43] Bloom is the "metropolitan type" *par excellence* who internalizes what he sees, hears, and feels in order to protect himself from the barrage of stimuli around him. As readers, we are privy to the numerous ways that these impressions translate into words and thoughts with each passing second.

Here is Bloom around 1.30 p.m.:

> His smile faded as he walked, a heavy cloud hiding the sun slowly, shadowing Trinity's surly front. Trams passed one another, ingoing, outgoing, clanging. Useless words. Things go on same, day after day: squads of police marching out, back: trams in, out. Those two loonies mooching about. Dignam carted off. Mina Purefoy swollen belly on a bed groaning to have a child tugged out of her. One born every second somewhere. Other dying every second. Since I fed the birds five minutes. Three hundred kicked the bucket. Other three hundred born, washing the blood off, all are washed in the blood of the lamb, bawling maaaaaa. (*U*, 8: 475–83)

As Bloom's body moves through Dublin, his mind fixes on the external environment and transforms it into a series of associations and reflections. Here, for instance, the cloud that covers the sun, combined with the sight and sound of the tram-cars, inspires Bloom's thoughts on the cycle of life and death which, for him at that moment, are associated with Paddy Dignam and Mina Purefoy. His mind quickly leaps from Mina Purefoy's painful labor (three days) to the handbill that he was handed earlier announcing "Elijah is coming. Dr John Alexander Dowie restorer of the church of Zion is coming" (*U*, 8: 13–14). Bloom's mind will turn to these same thoughts at various other points throughout the day. What makes them unique each time are the way that Bloom manages to rope them together. The timetable of tram-cars can refer metaphorically to the cycle of life, five minutes can mean that three hundred people have died while three hundred others have been born. Later on, tram-cars, pregnancy, and Paddy Dignam will spur on an entirely different sequence of thoughts. It will take some getting used to, but with each passing episode, patterns do emerge.

Although Bloom avoids going home until the wee hours of June 17, his mind never strays very far from Molly. The smallest detail can trigger memories of their life together, and he struggles throughout the day to keep himself distracted. At one moment his reflections on the universe lead to thoughts of a new moon, which he immediately associates with the first touch between Molly and Blazes: "Wait. The full moon was the night we were Sunday fortnight exactly there is the new moon. Walking down by the Tolka. Not bad for a Fairview moon. She was humming. The young May moon she's beaming, love. He other side of her. Elbow, arm. Glowworm's la-amp is gleaming, love. Touch. Fingers. Asking. Answer. Yes" (*U*, 8: 587–91). Bloom combines the verses from Thomas Moore's "Young May Moon" with a covert touch between Molly and Boylan. His memory of Boylan's first touch with Molly cleverly anticipates Molly's memory of Bloom's first kiss in the final line of her soliloquy with the same sequence of asking, answer, and yes. If Boylan's first touch leads to an act of betrayal, the memory of a consummated kiss at the novel's close may suggest the possibility for recovery and renewal in the future.

Bloom's allroundness becomes apparent through his memories of the past and his anxieties about the future. If Stephen is haunted by a dead mother, Bloom is haunted by a dead father and son. His father, Rudolph Virag (later changed to Bloom after he emigrated from Hungary to Dublin), committed suicide in the Queen's Hotel in Cork on 27 June 1886. His son's sudden death in 1894 put an end to his sexual relations with Molly. These incidents have dramatically shaped who Bloom is by the time we find him on 16 June 1904. He feels tremendous guilt for both deaths, and he is caught between his obligations as a father, son, and husband. As much as he remembers the woolly coat they buried Rudy in, he also recalls the image of his lonely father: "An old man, widower, unkempt of hair, in bed, with head covered, sighing: an infirm dog, Athos: aconite, resorted to by increasing doses of grains and scruples as a palliative of recrudescent neuralgia: the face in death of a septuagenerian, suicide by poison" (*U*, 17: 1889–92).

He is planning to travel to a memorial service for his father the following week instead of accompanying Molly to her concert in Belfast with Boylan. In the immediate present and the not-so-distant future, Bloom needs to define his role as a father to Milly and a husband to Molly. Confronting him at the beginning of the day is the question of whether or not he can stop Milly from growing up and keep Molly from cheating on him: "Molly. Milly. Same thing watered down" (*U*, 6: 87). After rereading Milly's letter that morning, he considers the possible sexual indiscretions of mother and daughter alike: "O, well: she knows how to mind herself. But if not? No, nothing has happened. Of course it might. Wait in any case till it does. A wild piece of goods. Her slim legs running up the staircase. Destiny. Ripening now. Vain: very" (*U*, 4: 428–31).

The conflation of mother and daughter, like that of father and son, brings us to a key philosophical question in *Ulysses*. How can an individual be one and many at the same time? These are the questions Stephen poses in the National Library when he asks how Shakespeare could be both Hamlet the father and Hamlet the son. For Molly, though, she wants an answer in "plain words" and with Bloom she gets it through his definition of "metempsychosis": "Metempsychosis, he said, is what the ancient Greeks called it. They used to believe you could be changed into an animal or a tree, for instance. What they called nymphs for example" (*U*, 4: 375–77). The ancient Greeks, Bloom explains, believed that reincarnation made the soul immortal. In *Ulysses* metempsychosis is a way to explain how Bloom can be Ulysses, Stephen a distraught Telemachus (or Hamlet), and Molly an unfaithful Penelope.

Metempsychosis has another more practical meaning for each of these characters. Am I now what I once was? Or was I then what I am now? In their own particular ways, Molly, Stephen, and Bloom feel unfulfilled in their lives, and their minds turn at one point or another to the possibility that happiness has passed them by. Thinking back to the time before Rudy was born, Bloom wonders: "I was happier then. Or was that I? Or am I now I? Twenty-eight I was. She twenty-three. When we left Lombard street west something changed. Could never like it again after Rudy. Can't bring back time. Like holding water in your hand" (*U*, 8: 608–11). Molly seems more certain that their relationship took a turn for the worst after Rudy's death: "I suppose I oughtn't to have buried him in that little woolly jacket I knitted crying as I was but give it to some poor child but I knew well Id never have another our 1st death too it was we were never the same since" (*U*, 18: 1448–50). Thinking back to his days as an altar boy at Clongowes Wood College, Stephen thinks, "I am another now and yet the same. A servant too. A server of a servant" (*U*, 1: 311–12). Later on, he thinks of using the identity-in-flux argument to get out of repaying a loan to George Russell, who goes by the initials "AE": "Wait. Five months. Molecules all change. I am other I now. Other I got pound . . . But I, entelechy, form of forms, am I by memory because of everchanging forms . . . I, I and I. A.E.I.O.U" (*U*, 9: 205–213).

Bloom is curious about everything. His mind constantly wavers between thoughts of Dublin's streets and more cosmic questions about the stars above. Part of his charm comes from his strong sense of compassion for others and his desire to see the world as others see it. Looking down at his cat, he wonders, "They call them stupid. They understand what we say better than we understand them. She understands all she wants to" (*U*, 4: 26–27). Following behind the blind stripling later that afternoon, he thinks: "Look at all the things they can learn to do. Read with their fingers. Tune pianos. Or are we surprised they have any brains. Why we think a deformed person or a hunchback clever if he says something we might say" (*U*, 8: 1115–17). Bloom sympathizes with the outsiders, or dark horses, because he is one. Raised by an Ashkenazi Hungarian father and an Irish mother, Bloom is a hybrid, both Irish, Jewish, and, interestingly, belonging completely to neither category. He is the foreigner inside the Irish nation, and his status as a Jew is fraught with serious contradictions: he has been baptized twice, he does not have a Jewish mother, and he has not been circumcised. In "Ithaca" when we get the question of Bloom's thoughts about Stephen's thoughts about Bloom, we get an equally confusing response: "He thought that he thought that he was a jew whereas he knew that he knew that he knew he was not" (*U*, 17: 530–31). There are a number of positions that critics have taken to try to resolve this question once and for all. What seems to matter most of all is the idea that Bloom identifies himself as a Jew.

Asked why he chose to have a Jewish protagonist in *Ulysses*, Joyce responded, "Yes, because only a foreigner would do. The Jews were foreigners at that time. There was no hostility toward them, but contempt, yes, the contempt people always show for the unknown."[44] If Joyce first became interested in exile for artists and Irishmen, his thoughts on the subject broadened to include an even more ancient history. Although Joyce reads Irish national deliverance in terms of the Jewish diaspora, many of his characters refuse to entertain such a comparative historical perspective. As a result, we find Bloom on a number of occasions subject directly and indirectly to the anti-Semitic rants of his fellow citizens.

Bloom's reticence during these moments should not be confused with silent resignation. He is a pacifist by nature, and his greatest challenge arises when he encounters the nameless narrator, Joe Hynes, the Citizen, and the nationalist mutt Garryowen in Barney Kiernan's pub. As with Ulysses, he is a "nobody" (*outis*), but instead of a hungry Cyclops, he has to deal with narrow-minded nationalists. Up until this episode, set between five and six o'clock, Bloom has not explicitly defended either his Irishness or his Jewishness. In "Cyclops," he is forced to do both. In Bloom's presence the Citizen rants and raves about the persecution of the Irish race and the glory of a lost civilization on the verge of a national awakening. In the most grandiloquent style, the nameless narrator describes the Citizen wearing a girdle of seastones with graven images of "Irish heroes and heroines of antiquity": included among them are Napoleon Bonaparte, Julius Caesar, Muhammad, Ludwig Beethoven, and Dante Alighieri. These men may well have been heroes, but they certainly were not Irish. The girdle provides an ironic commentary on the Citizen's message: he wants a pure Irish race, which does not exist, and a mythical past that gives Ireland a prominent place in the history of the world.

The Citizen cannot see Irish history within the broader continuum of human history that includes the constant intermixing of races, cultures, histories, and tongues. Persecution, as Bloom reminds him, is not only an Irish phenomenon: "the history of the world is full of it. Perpetuating national hatred among nations" (*U*, 12: 1417–18). Asked if he knows what a nation is, Bloom responds, "A nation is the same people living in the same place," slipping in the proviso, "Or also living in different places" (*U*, 12: 1422–23, 1428). For the Citizen, the nation is land-based and belonging or not belonging depends upon whether or not one lives or does not live within its borders. Not so for Bloom. His own identity as the persecuted Jew ("I belong to a race too . . . that is hated and persecuted") and the Irishman ("I was born here. Ireland") has given him a dual-consciousness existing inside and outside the strict definitions of an Irish nation or an Irish identity.

Bloom infuriates the Citizen by telling him that his own religion was not as pure, meaning non-Semitic, as he once believed: "And the Savior was a jew and his father was a jew. Your God . . . Well, his uncle was a jew, says he. Your God was a jew. Christ was a jew like me" (*U*, 12: 1805–09). Jews and Christians share the same history even if they disagree on whether or not Christ was the Savior. For the third time, Bloom counters the Citizen's single-mindedness by finding points of identification between histories, nations, and races instead of reasons for exclusion. The Citizen's views, though, are as fixed as the seastones on his girdle, and the myth of his own Irishness is itself dependent on his one-eyed belief in the purity of the Irish race.

We spend most of the novel following Bloom's adventures in the world, but like him, we are often left wondering what Molly is up to back home. Except for a few brief remarks in "Calypso," we do not get to hear what Molly has to say until the very last episode. Even though she is rarely seen or heard for most of the novel, her presence is felt everywhere. It was the same problem that Joyce worked out with Beatrice in Act 2 of *Exiles*. As he reflected in one of his notes for the play, she is not on stage but "her figure must appear before the audience through the thoughts or speech of others" (*E*, 174). The same is true in *Ulysses*, but the delay is even more attenuated.

Molly's four o'clock rendezvous with Boylan, which coincides with the "Sirens" episode, is the absent center of the novel. After seeing Boylan's letter earlier that morning, Bloom believes that their appointment to "rehearse" for an upcoming concert is really an opportunity for sex. Instead of staying at home for the day or interrupting them at four o'clock when Boylan is supposed to visit her, he lets it happen. This is the same kind of adulterous triangle that Joyce worked out in *Exiles* when Richard leaves Robert alone with Bertha in Act 2: the tryst, if there ever is one in the case of *Exiles*, takes place offstage.

"Sirens" represents a displaced seduction scene. Between the hours of four and five o'clock we know that something is supposed to happen back at 7 Eccles Street. Instead of setting the scene where the action is, we are at the Ormond Hotel where Bloom meets Richie Goulding (Stephen's uncle) for an early dinner. As is the case with Bloom's masturbation on the beach in "Nausicaa," we do not see a thing. In the early part of the episode we watch Miss Lydia Douce and Miss Kennedy, the bronze and gold mermaids/barmaids, flirt with the clientele. In the place of a voyeuristic peek into the bedroom, we get Miss Douce working suggestively at the beerpull as Ben Dollard sings "The Croppy Boy":

> On the smooth jutting beerpull laid Lydia hand, plumply, leave it to my hands. All lost in pity for croppy. Fro, to: to, fro: over the polished knob (she knows his eyes, my eyes, her eyes) her thumb and finger passed in pity: passed, reposed and, gently touching, then slid so smoothly, slowly down, a cool firm white enamel baton protruding through her sliding ring. With a cock with a carra. Tap. Tap. Tap. (*U*, 11: 1112–17)

The seduction in "Sirens" is one of the ear and not the eye. Instead of seeing what happens between Molly and Boylan, Joyce keeps the focus on Bloom's troubled mind. Everything he hears during this hour reminds him of Molly's impending infidelity. Bloom is particularly despondent when he listens to Ben Dollard sing "Tutto è sciolto" ("All is lost now") from Vincenzo Bellini's *La Sonnambula*. It recounts the story of a man who falsely believes that his fiancée has cheated on him while sleepwalking. Unlike the man in the opera, Bloom expects his wife to be wide awake for her affair. He imagines Molly's unfaithfulness in terms of a symbolic fall, one that he still thinks, if only for a minute, he might prevent: "Fall, surrender, lost . . . Yes, I remember. Lovely air. In sleep she went to him. Innocence of the moon. Brave. Don't know their danger. Still hold her back. Call name. Touch water. Jingle Jaunty. Too late. She longed to go. That's why. Woman. As easy to stop the sea. Yes: all is lost" (*U*, 11: 636–41).

When he leaves the Ormond Hotel, the affair between Molly and Boylan is presumably in progress. The time to intervene has passed, and Bloom now walks Dublin's streets as the cuckolded husband. So far he has not provided any musical accompaniment, but as the episode comes to a close he reads the words of the Irish patriot Robert Emmet in a shop window and adds his own flatulent flourish:

> Seabloom, greaseabloom viewed last words. Softly. *When my country takes her place among.* Prrprr. Must be the bur. Fff! Oo. Rrpr. *Nations of the earth.* No-one behind. She's passed. *Then and not till then.* Tram

> kran kran kran. Good oppor. Coming. Krandlkrankran. I'm sure it's the
> burgund. Yes. One, two. *Let my epitaph be.* Kraaaaaa. *Written. I have.*
> Pprrpffrrppffff. *Done.* (*U*, 11: 1284–94)

In this final instance, "done" can refer to the passing of a tram, Emmet's
words, and Bloom's fart. It can also refer back to the deed done back home,
one that can no longer be undone. As tragic as the affair might seem to
Bloom, his fart lends a comic note as well. Regardless of what will happen
with him and Molly in the future, life goes on.[45]

Although we watch the psychological effects of the affair on Bloom during
"Sirens," we get a glimpse into some possible motivations for why he let it
happen in "Circe." After bumping into a drunken Stephen in the Holles Street
Hospital, where he has gone to find out about Mina Purefoy, Bloom follows
him to Bella Cohen's brothel in Nighttown. This episode presents a sequence of
strange hallucinations that provide a rare peek into Bloom's unconscious. In
one of them he watches Boylan and Molly through a keyhole. He is not
troubled by what he sees. Instead, he eggs them on: "(*his eyes wildly dilated,
clasps himself*) Show! Hide! Show! Plough her! More! Shoot!" (*U*, 15: 3814–15).
The hallucination indicates, at least for one psychoanalytically charged reading, that as impotent and powerless as Bloom may feel in the face of Boylan's
exaggerated virility, he also feels somewhat responsible and more than a little
turned on. Instead of being a helpless victim, this imagined peek through
the keyhole reveals that he is an indirect participant in his wife's indiscretions.

In the "Ithaca" episode, which is presented in the form of a question and
answer session or a Catholic catechism, we find out that Bloom thinks Boylan
is only the most recent addition to a long line of lovers that include Simon
Dedalus and an Italian organ-grinder. Except for Lieutenant Mulvey, Molly's
"first kiss," he is dead wrong. For the first time, we also get a straightforward
account of what Bloom thinks of Boylan:

> What were his reflections concerning the last member of this series and
> late occupant of the bed?
>
> Reflections on his vigour (a bounder), corporal proportion (a
> billsticker), commercial ability (a bester), impressionability (a boaster).
> (*U*, 17: 2143–46)

Bloom is not angry with Boylan or Molly. Instead, he is more preoccupied
with what will happen to his marriage in the future. The thought of divorce
crosses his mind ("Divorce, not now"), but it is clear that Bloom still loves
and is attracted to Molly. When he crawls into bed with her, he notices
crumbs and a dry semen stain. With his face at her buttocks, he kisses

"the plump mellow yellow smellow melons of her rump" before falling asleep (*U*, 17: 2241). After a long day wandering around Dublin, our hero is finally home: "He rests, he has traveled" (*U*, 17: 2320).

Once Bloom falls asleep, Molly's own journey begins. Between "Ithaca" and "Penelope," Bloom has presumably asked Molly to make him breakfast in the morning.[46] His request is not recorded directly in the novel, but Molly's puzzled response in the very first line of "Penelope" is "Yes because he never did a thing like that before as ask to get his breakfast in bed" (*U*, 18: 1). As with most things in *Ulysses*, this request means more than it says. His request for breakfast in bed, if he did make one, would suggest that Bloom is asserting himself. But if he did not make the request, we might surmise that Molly wants to hear one so that she can make breakfast as an act of reconciliation. Regardless of whether he said it or not, Molly seems willing to play along: "Ill throw him up his eggs and tea in the moustachecup" (*U*, 18: 1504–05). She even thinks of giving him a bit more: "Ill put on my best shift and drawers let him have a good eyeful out of that to make his micky stand for him" (*U*, 18: 1509–10).

"Penelope" is one long soliloquy with eight periods and no other punctuation. It was Joyce's first attempt to represent the mind of a woman (he will do it again at the end of *Finnegans Wake* with the meditation of Anna Livia Plurabelle). The intimate thoughts of Molly Bloom in "Penelope" should not be confused with an unmediated peek into the female mind. It is one male author's projection of what he thinks, or wants to think, women think. Although the know-it-all narrator in "Ithaca" tells us that Bloom finds crumbs and a human imprint "not his", Molly gives us a more explicit description: "he must have come 3 or 4 times with that tremendous big red brute of a thing" (*U*, 17: 2124, 18: 143–44). Boylan was not the only one to have fun: "O Lord I must stretch myself I wished he was here or somebody to let myself go with and come again like that I feel all fire inside me or if I could dream it when he made me spend the 2nd time tickling me behind with his finger I was coming for about 5 minutes with my legs around him" (*U*, 18: 584–87).

Molly's monologue confirms and revises a lot of what we hear about her in the previous episodes. We know, of course, what Bloom thinks, but her fellow citizens also have an opinion. Everyone in Dublin seems to know what Molly and Boylan are up to. During almost every encounter Bloom has, Molly's name comes up. On two separate occasions M'Coy and Nosey Flynn ask the same question: "Who's getting it up?" (*U*, 5: 153, 8: 73). Boylan is behind these questions: he will be "getting it on" and "getting it up" later in the afternoon. However, while she does think a lot about sex, Molly is not as promiscuous as everyone seems to think. When Lenehan talks to M'Coy earlier in the day, he claims that Molly accepted his advances one evening in a crowded cab: "Every jolt the bloody car gave I had her bumping up against me. Hell's delights! She has a fine pair, God bless her. Like that" (*U*, 10: 558–60). From Molly, we get quite a different story: "that sponger [Lenehan] he was making free with me after the Glencree dinner coming back that long joult over the featherbed mountain" (*U*, 18: 426–27).

As much as we learn about Boylan's prowess in the bedroom, we also find out that Molly finds him a bit vulgar. She did not like the fact that he "slapped her behind," and she "halfshut" her own eyes at one point to avoid his "vicious look" during sex (*U*, 18: 122, 154). Molly also provides one final perspective on Bloom. She knows that the others "talk behind his back," and she is onto the fact that he is writing letters to someone else. She even suspects that he knows about Boylan and deliberately sent Milly away to Mullingar for the summer so that the affair could take place: "only hed do a thing like that all the same on account of me and Boylan thats why he did it Im certain the way he plots and plans everything" (*U*, 18: 1007–09).

As much as her romp with Boylan satisfied her sexually and may in the immediate future, she still seems to really care about Bloom and even blames him for the affair. It would be difficult to imagine that Molly feels guilty, but she does try to deflect the blame: "its all his own fault if I am an adultress" (*U*, 18: 1516). As with all Joyce's endings, it is not entirely clear if Molly and Bloom will stay together. 17 June might be a new beginning for them, but it might also be the beginning of the end. Molly, after all, is still planning to go to Belfast with Boylan and she even toys with the idea of a sexual romp on the train. And Bloom, so far as we know, is still planning to let it happen.

Before drifting off to sleep, Molly remembers when Bloom first proposed to her on Howth head. It is a memory confusingly mixed with her first sexual experience as a young girl back in Gibraltar with Harry Mulvey, a lieutenant in the Royal Navy:

> yes and all the queer little streets and the pink and blue and yellow houses and the rosegardens and the Jessamine and geraniums and cactuses and Gibraltar as a girl where I was Flower of the mountain yes when I put the rose in my hair like the Andalusian girls used or shall I wear a red yes and how he kissed me under the Moorish wall and I thought well as well him as another and then I asked him with my eyes to ask again yes and then he asked me would I yes to say yes my mountain flower and first I put my arms around him yes and drew him down to me so he could feel my breasts all perfume yes and his heart was going like mad and yes I said yes I will Yes. (*U*, 18: 1599–1609)

Even if you have never read *Ulysses*, you may have come across this passage in some form or another. It is one of the more contested passages in Joyce's works. The sleepy Molly is mixing two memories together here: one of her first kiss with Lieutenant Mulvey under the Moorish wall in Gibraltar when she was still a young girl, and the other of Bloom's proposal to her. Is Molly responding to the memory of Mulvey's first kiss or Bloom's proposal? Earlier on in the chapter, she had already associated Mulvey with flowers and the sensation of his body against her breasts (*U*, 18: 773–75). Her final "Yes" may signify a triumphant acceptance of her life with Bloom, an affirmative and silent renewal of her vow to him. But if Molly is to be identified with a circumspect Penelope, who spins her yarn by day and unspins it by night, it is impossible to know if her final sleepy words can be trusted.

Finnegans Wake

When Joyce finished writing *Ulysses*, he was not sure what to do next. He had exhausted the English language, revolutionized the form of the novel, and inserted himself forcefully into the annals of literary history. Despite these unique achievements, he was determined to take his experiments with language and literary form even further. By March 1923, roughly a year after *Ulysses* was published, he had jotted down the first two pages for his next book. Thus began a process that would occupy him for sixteen years. Joyce devoted half of his creative life to what he referred to in public as *Work in Progress* and in private with Nora as *Finnegans Wake*. The official title was released only when the book itself was published. *Finnegans Wake* was the book he had been working toward since *Dubliners*. It was the one he wanted to be remembered for. Even the most fanatical readers of the *Wake* will admit that a lifetime is barely enough to understand this "meanderthalltale," a meandering tall-tale (*FW*, 19.25). *Finnegans Wake* can take a lifetime of dedicated study, but there are a number of possibilities for those brave souls willing to give it a short-term shot. Readers who refuse to be daunted by bouts of incomprehension will find the experience rewarding and, at times, hilarious. All first, second, or third timers should approach *Finnegans Wake* with a sense of humour. "I am nothing but an Irish clown," Joyce once said about himself, "a great joker at the universe."[47]

At an early stage, as parts of *Finnegans Wake* were appearing in serial form, H. G. Wells complained that Joyce had forgotten the "common reader":

> You have turned your back on common men, on their elementary
> needs and their restricted time and intelligence and you have

> elaborated. What is the result? Vast riddles. . . . So I ask: Who the hell is
> this Joyce who demands so many waking hours of the few thousands
> I have still to live for a proper appreciation of his quirks and fancies and
> flashes of rendering (*LI*, 275).

You might end up asking yourself "who the hell" this Joyce is, but you might
still find it worth while to devote at least some "waking hours" to reading
Finnegans Wake. Despite Wells's admonition, it really is a book that everyone
can enjoy. Some claim that if you come across your name (or initials) on any
of the pages, you were destined to read it (I found mine): I encourage you to
give it a shot. Whether by way of astral interference, class requirements, or
just plain curiosity, the decision to read *Finnegans Wake* is a big one that will
require time, effort, and some patience.

People who know the book by reputation alone wonder how to get started.
The short answer: read it! The most appropriate introduction to the *Wake* is the
Wake. As disorienting as the experience can be at first, it does get easier as you go
along.[48] It is tempting to consult the secondary literature right off the bat, but it
is better, I think, to read it through from beginning to end or at least try a section
or two. If you try to interpret every word, you will get bogged down thinking
about how much you do not know. It also helps to read in small doses, a couple
of pages at a time at the beginning so that you do not get too frustrated.

Finnegans Wake is not a page-turner like *Great Expectations*. It resists many
of the responses and identifications that we often associate with novel
reading. The endless play of the language, more than a suspenseful plot, is
what drives you forward. As a way to get your bearings, it is helpful to keep a list
of words, phrases, sentences, and rhythms that catch your eye or ear. Depending
on your interests and background, you will certainly find something that
interests you. Some have even claimed that the book predicts the coming of
Elvis Presley! There are a number of literary, biblical, and historical allusions, as
one might expect with Joyce, but readers will also find jokes and songs in more
than sixty different languages (maybe more). The Dublin postal directory from
1904 gave him the names of sixty Dublin mayors for one passage. When writing
the "Anna Livia Plurabelle" (I.viii.) chapter and "Haveth Childers Everywhere"
(II, 532.1–554.10) section, Joyce gleaned hundreds of river and city names from
the *Encyclopedia Britannica*. If "Slutsgarten" sounds familiar, you probably have
some knowledge of Christiania (capital of Norway and home to the playwright
Henrik Ibsen) where "Slotspark" can be found (*FW*, 532.22). Since there is no
linear narrative, none of the traditional novelistic trappings that demarcate a
beginning, middle, and end, a cast of easily recognizable characters, or a plot, it is
possible to start anywhere.

Because of its encyclopedic scope and mix of languages, some think that a polyglot group of global readers is the best way to read *Finnegans Wake*. But whether you are in a group (virtual or real) or alone, you can enjoy it. Sometimes it helps to read words or passages out loud (a recommendation Joyce once made to a puzzled reader). Even if the words look completely foreign, they will often sound familiar once you actually pronounce them. Here is how the "soundsense and sensesound" of *Finnegans Wake* sometimes works (*FW*, 121.15). "Pee ess," "so vi et," "Hereweareagain," and "crossmess parzel," for instance, might look unintelligible on the page, but they sound like "P.S.," "Soviet," "Here we are again," and "Christmas parcel" when you speak them (*FW*, 111.18, 414.14, 455.25, 619.5). Part of the fun of *Finnegans Wake* is finding out that you can hear what Joyce means.

There are some basics to *Finnegans Wake* (plot, character, themes and motifs, structure, and language) that this introduction will give you, but they are largely provisional. If anything, they are intended to function as signposts that will point you in some possible directions. Even the specialists are still arguing over what the book is "about": Is it a dream? Is there a single person dreaming? What does and does not happen? The literary conventions that most readers expect when they open up a book have disappeared or are barely discernible. It does help to have some knowledge of Joyce's earlier works. Even he claimed that *Finnegans Wake* represented a continuation of what he had begun with *Dubliners*:

> Each of my books is a book about Dublin. Dublin is a city of scarcely three hundred thousand population, but it has become the universal city of my work. *Dubliners* was my last look at that city. Then I looked at the people around me. *Portrait* was the picture of my spiritual self. *Ulysses* transformed individual impressions and emotions to give them general significance. "Work in Progress" has a significance completely above reality; transcending humans, things, sense, and entering the realm of complete abstraction.[49]

When he first began to compile material for *Finnegans Wake*, he consulted the twelve kilos of notes he had left over from *Ulysses*. He also began to organize words and phrases under the titles of his previous works in his *Scribbledehobble* notebook. Some believe that *Finnegans Wake* begins where *Ulysses* ends, with Leopold and Molly fast asleep. Joyce even referred to *Ulysses* in an offhand remark as "a little prelude to 'Work in Progress.'"[50] The stream of consciousness (defined loosely here as the free association of thought) that characterized Molly's soliloquy gives way to what Harry Levin first called the "stream of unconsciousness."[51]

For better or for worse, there was no great explicator to *Finnegans Wake* when Joyce was still alive as there had been for *Ulysses* (though many suspect that Joyce was priming his friend Jacques Mercanton for the job shortly before he died). In the few articles that he surreptitiously supervised and in the letters that survive, however, we get some sense of what the book meant to him. Nowadays we are suspicious of relying on authorial intentions for textual interpretations. But if we acknowledge that *Finnegans Wake* encourages a plurality of interpretations, we should also acknowledge that the author himself had some that might be of use. Joyce's initial explanations began to emerge when friends and detractors alike bemoaned his latest experiment in the late 1920s. Once on the defensive, he came up with theories that he channeled through a coterie of friends and critics. Particularly popular was the "dream theory," which continues to have widespread appeal.

Joyce was well aware that he had a strange connection with the founding father of psychoanalysis, Sigmund Freud, who had his own theory about dreams. Freud in German and Joyce in English mean the same thing: joy. As suspicious as Joyce was of Freud's work, perhaps because he was such a powerful influence, he was not averse to treating *Finnegans Wake* as a kind of dream world. Long before writing it, Joyce kept a series of dream books in which he recorded and interpreted the dreams of family members and friends, and he used a number of psychoanalytic concepts about the unconscious to develop the "Circe" episode of *Ulysses*. Freud definitely had an impact on the way Joyce understood the unconscious, but he always claimed that he preferred the work of the seventeenth-century Neapolitan philosopher Giambattista Vico, who had his own theory on the relationship between language and mythology, which I will say more about shortly.

In defense of his book's obscurity, Joyce told Harriet Shaw Weaver that he was representing a nocturnal state, "which cannot be rendered sensible by the use of wideawake language, cutandry grammar and goahead plot" (*SL*, 318). Several years later, Frank Budgen (author of *James Joyce and the Making of "Ulysses"*, 1934) and several other contributors to *Our Exagmination Round His Factification for Incamination of "Work in Progress"* (1929) played up the dream motif. In his essay Budgen makes the charge that *Finnegans Wake* cannot be understood without it:

> Whatever the elements brought together they have the rightness of a
> dream wherein all things we ever knew or experienced occur not in their
> time sequence but according to their necessary importance in the
> pattern dictated by the dream's own purpose and logic. And this I take
> to be the key to the understanding of *Work in Progress* and the secret of

its peculiar beauty. In *Ulysses* is the life–the real life–of day; here the reality–super reality–of night.[52]

If you read *Finnegans Wake* as a dream, or rather as the literary rendering of a dream, then you can treat the various plots, narrative structures, and characters as manifestations of what a dream might seem like. Whatever you choose to do, it is worth knowing that "the dream" had been produced by a history of critical interpretation (beginning with Joyce himself) and functions much like the Homeric correspondences did for *Ulysses*: it is a scaffolding that the author needed in order to rationalize, and in some sense organize, the meaning of his work.[53]

To get a sense of *Finnegans Wake* as a whole, it is worth having some idea of how Joyce wrote it. In 1924 the first piece of Joyce's "Work in Progress" appeared in the *transatlantic review,* and other sections followed sporadically in other journals. The serialization of the individual bits and pieces gave Joyce a series of deadlines that would keep him from getting lost in his own creation. The more intensive serial publication of *Finnegans Wake* began in *transition* in April 1927 and with a few interruptions Books I and III and parts of Book II appeared in 1928, 1929, 1933, 1935, 1937 and 1938. It was not long, however, before Joyce got word that many of his readers found his experimental work incomprehensible. Stanislaus accused his brother of "Literary bolshevism." His father humorously observed that his son "speaks better than he writes" (*LI*, 235). Most troubling to Joyce was the fact that Harriet Show Weaver began to cool off, suspecting that he was "wasting his genius" (*JJ*, 590). Despite his earlier support, Pound, too, was unwilling to be won over: "Nothing so far as I make out, nothing short of divine vision or a new cure for the clap can possibly be worth all the circumambient peripherization."[54] With two of his most loyal supporters falling by the wayside, Joyce was seriously depressed. He thought of passing on his work to another Irishman, Paul Stephens, but soon realized that he was the only one cut out for the job.

Although he began writing sections of "Work in Progress" in 1923, he did not have a structure in place for the whole book until 1928 or so. Instead of working chronologically from beginning to end, he often wrote and revised several different sections at a time. As with *Ulysses,* he was ushering in changes up until the very last minute and letting his book develop according to an accretive revision process. His friend Louis Gillet explained that "he [Joyce] tackled it from all angles, a little here, a little there. He did not write it all in one breath, beginning at the first line, but worked on the fragment that suited him at the moment, leaving blank spaces."[55] This diachronic method of composition, the constant going back and forth between sections, freed

Joyce in many ways from the formal restrictions of a linear design. Instead, he treated *Finnegans Wake* as a kind of mosaic whose overall shape was in place, with a design that gradually came into focus. It was a process, he believed, triggered as much by chance as calculation. "Chance," he told Mercanton, "furnishes me what I need. I am like a man who stumbles along: my foot strikes something, I bend over, and it is exactly what I want."[56]

Chance may have played an important role in the composition of *Finnegans Wake*, but Joyce did have some structures in place to organize his material. He chose a four-book structure for *Finnegans Wake* (like the four stages of *Dubliners*). It was based on the three stages of history (gods, heroes, and humans) followed by a *ricorso*, or transition into chaos, outlined by Vico. Joyce first read Vico's *New Science* when he was in Trieste and always maintained an interest in this cyclical view of history. In *New Science* Vico argued, among other things, that the study of language and mythology were keys for understanding the course of human history.[57] Of particular interest to Joyce was Vico's idea that history is made by human beings. By analyzing myth and the etymologies of words, it was possible to determine the various patterns of human behavior and uncover the presence of the collective personalities that define individual ages. References to these three stages and the *ricorso* can be found throughout *Finnegans Wake*, but they also correspond with a number of other themes that he was working with: original sin, the fall, birth, marriage, death, and resurrection.

The title, *Finnegans Wake*, comes from an Irish-American ballad that also follows the cycle of life, death, and resurrection. In it a hod-carrier by the name of Tim Finnegan falls from a ladder to his death. During the wake, the smell of whiskey revives him (or whiskey is spilled on him, depending on the version), and he rises from the coffin to join the party. As was the case with Leopold Bloom, Tim Finnegan is at once an Irishman and an everyman. He is a composite of the Irish legendary hero Finn MacCool, Adam, King Mark of the Tristan and Isolde legend, Noah, Richard III, Napoleon, and Parnell. For his own version, *Finnegans Wake*, Joyce omitted the apostrophe to include everyone, and he found in these two words the themes of birth, fall, death, and resurrection. The French *fin* ("end") and the English *again* ("another beginning") precede the *wake*, which simultaneously denotes a deathwatch and a resurrection.

Moving from the title to the first sentence, you find a number of these themes and structures already in place: "riverrun, past Eve and Adam's, from swerve of shore to bend of bay, brings us by a commodius vicus of recirculation back to Howth Castle and Environs" (*FW*, 3.1–3).[58] Continued from the novel's final words ("A way a lone a last a loved a long the"), there is a river running its course, a reference to Adam and Eve (which is also the name of a church) and Vico (vicus), a place (Howth Castle and Environs), and, as you will soon find out, a character, whose initials (HCE) are embedded in the capitalized letters of the place. The book is already in progress, but its beginning goes as far back as Genesis or the first stage of Vico's cycle of history. In the third paragraph, there is "the fall" followed by one hundred letters in parentheses signifying the sound of thunder.[59] The first chapter of Book I is a good place to get acclimatized since so many of the central motifs occur and recur: original sin, falling, sleeping, waking, and rising. The multiple references to Dublin in Chapter 1 ("Doublin," "Dobbelin," "Dbln," "durblin," "Humblin," "delvin," "Doublends," "doublejoynted," "*Dybbling*") are a constant reminder that as universal as Joyce's history of the world may be, it is firmly anchored in Ireland (*FW*, 3.8, 7.12, 13.14, 19.12, 18.6, 21.6, 20.16, 27.2, 29.22). "Dyoublong?" is a question every reader is forced to ask, since references to Irish folklore, history, geography, and myth abound (*FW*, 13.4).

Finnegans Wake may begin with the fall of Tim Finnegan (or of Adam and Eve or Humpty Dumpty, depending on how you read it), but it soon gives way to a newcomer, who will dominate the rest of the book. He is a character of sorts, but not the kind you might be used to. As Joyce once explained it, "There are, so to say, no individual people in the book–it is in a dream, the style gliding and unreal as is the way in dreams. If one were to speak of a person in the book, it would have to be of an old man, but even his relationship to reality is doubtful."[60] "Humphrey Chimpden Earwicker" is his "official" name. He also goes by the initials HCE, which are often embedded in sequences of words that begin or end with these letters. He can be "Hush! Caution! Echoland!," "Hag, Chivychas Eve," "HeCitEncy," "Her Chuff Exsquire!," and "Health, chalce, endnessnessessity" (*FW*, 13.5, 30.14, 421.23, 205.22, 613.27). In reverse, he is "Eusbian Concordant Homilies" (*FW*, 409.36).

The surname, "Earwicker," is associated with the "earwig," an insect which, according to superstition, would crawl into people's ears as they slept. In Irish-English "earwigging" is slang for "gossip," and a lot is said about HCE throughout the book. He is a tavernkeeper and family man living in Chapelizod (a suburb outside Dublin), but he has been suspected of a crime in Phoenix Park. He might have spied on two girls while they were peeing, exposed himself, or thought of them while masturbating. There are three soldiers, who claim that they saw something, though they are never sure exactly what. Whatever HCE did becomes a matter of public interest after he nervously (and with a stutter) recounts his entire past to an old Cad in Phoenix Park, who innocently asks him the time. After the Cad returns home and tells his wife, who in turn tells a priest, the rumor takes off all over Dublin. By the end of the second chapter of Book II, there is already a song circulating about HCE, who is referred to as "Persse O'Reilly" ("perce-oreille" is French for "earwig").

Other members of the Earwicker family include HCE's wife, Anna Livia Plurabelle (ALP); his twin sons, Shem the rebel artist and Shaun the conformist postman; and his daughter Isabelle ("Issy" and "Izzy"). They are either independent characters from the waking world, or different manifestations of H.C.E.'s unconscious. Except for Issy, they are the subject of individual chapters: ALP in I.v., I.viii., and IV; Shem in I.vii.; Shaun in III.ii and iii. They also represent natural elements: HCE is a hill, ALP a river, Shem a tree, Shaun a stone, and Issy a cloud. In addition to the Earwicker family, there are twelve taverngoers, who represent the jurors at the trial or mourners at the wake, Kate the maid and Joe the handyman, the twenty-eight playmates of Issy, and the Four Old Men or Judges, who are also the four evangelists Matthew, Mark, Luke, and John (or Mamalujo). In the fourth chapter of Book III, as a new day begins to dawn, there are references to a Porter family (Mr. Porter, his wife Ann, his two sons Kevin and Jerry, and his daughter Isobel), who represent another possible incarnation of the Earwicker family. Some argue that Mr. Porter is the master dreamer, while others conclude that it would be impossible for any single consciousness to contain such an extended dream sequence.

The four books of *Finnegans Wake* are not an example of "continuarration!" (*FW*, 205.14). They do not follow a straightforward linear narrative. They are, however, organized around a number of "plots" and framed by a "wake" in Book I (of Tim Finnegan and HCE) and an "awakening" (of ALP) in Book IV. As with everything else in the *Wake*, there is no consensus on what happens in between. Critics will more readily agree, however, that the style of the *Wake* is structured around phases of relative clarity in Books I and IV and obscurity in Books II and III. The novel traces a gradual descent into the nightworld or dreamworld and the progressive obscurity signals the successive stages of waking and sleeping, day and night. Without restricting the four Books to a number of fixed interpretations, there are some general summaries that can help to guide your reading. Since what happens in the *Wake* is open to debate, they are merely provisional points that you can accept or reject as you see fit.

The first chapter of Book I is a preamble for the entire book that lays out some of the dominant motifs. It is a good place to get your bearings, but in many ways it is not directly connected with the "plots" and "characters" that follow. The subsequent seven chapters of Book I introduce us to the nocturnal world of HCE. In addition to finding out about HCE's mysterious crime in Phoenix Park

(Chapter 2) and the rumors that ensue, there is a trial that leads to his arrest and incarceration (Chapter 3). By Chapter 4, HCE is buried in Lough Neagh and begins to fade from view. The following four chapters are not unified by a central character, but they include a description of a mysterious letter unearthed by a hen in Phoenix Park and presumably written by ALP (Chapter 5), a quiz show that introduces all the characters (Chapter 6), a portrait of the artist Shem (Chapter 7), and two washerwomen gossiping about ALP (Chapter 8).

Book II is by far the most difficult section for readers to get through, and it represents the darkest part of the night. Joyce even complained that parts of it "came out like drops of blood" (*LI*, 295). In it, Shem, Shaun, Issy and her classmates are playing a game called "Angels and Devils" in which one child ("the devil") tries to guess the colour that the others ("the Angels") have chosen. Unable to find the right answer, Shem loses and retreats back into the darkness. When sending a copy to his daughter Lucia (who did a number of designs for a separate edition), Joyce wrote, "I like it very much. Lord knows what my prose means. In a word, it is pleasing to the ear" (*LI*, 341). In Chapter 2 the children are doing their homework. As a way of explaining it, Joyce told Frank Budgen that "the technique here is a reproduction of a schoolboy's (and schoolgirl's) old classbook complete with marginalia by the twins, who change sides at half time, footnotes by the girl (who doesn't), a Euclid diagram, funny drawings, etc." (*LI*, 406). These "Night Lessons," as Joyce called them, deal largely with the acquisition of knowledge. Chapter 3 (the longest and most complex chapter in the *Wake* and one of the last written) takes place in a tavern and marks the brief return of HCE, the tavernkeeper, who cleans up (and drinks up) after a rowdy band of drinkers departs. In Chapter 4 H.C.E. dreams (or not) about the legend of Tristan and Isolde.

Book III is devoted primarily to Shaun the postman. Unlike his brother Shem, Shaun is a respectable upstanding citizen, who delivers the post. He appears as Shaun, Juan, and Yawn. He denigrates his brother's character, delivers a sermon to Issy's friends, and defends himself against the Four Old Men. Early on, Joyce imagined each of the chapters in Book III as the "Watches of Shaun." To him at least, they represent "the description of a postman traveling backwards in the night through the events already narrated. It is narrated in the form of a *via crucis* of 14 stations but in reality is only a barrel rolling down the river Liffey" (*LI*, 214). If Book III is a kind of time-machine that revisits "events already narrated," it also represents a rewriting of the *Wake* itself in which the son, Shaun, becomes the father, HCE. In Chapter 4 one of the children screams in a nightmare and awakens a new character, Mr. Porter, who represents yet another possible manifestation of HCE. References to the approaching dawn suggest that a new day is about to begin and the book is about to end. Book IV is the *ricorso*, an extended narrative with no individual chapters. ALP, as the River Liffey, thinks about the past as she approaches her father, the Irish Sea. In this moving crescendo, morning arrives as ALP returns to her source. Turning back to the first page, you discover that she continues to wind her way through Dublin.

By 1938 most of *Finnegans Wake* was in galley proofs or draft form, but Joyce still needed to finish the final pages. As Anna Livia Plurabelle returns to the Irish Sea, there is an unmistakable heaviness and nostalgia. In every end Joyce managed to find a new beginning, and he decided that the final line was best left without a full stop. The final word, however, was another story:

> In *Ulysses*, in order to convey the mumbling of a woman falling asleep, I wanted to finish with the faintest word that I could possibly discover. I found the word *yes*, which is barely pronounced, which implies consent, abandonment, relaxation, the end of all resistance. For "Work in Progress" I tried something better if possible. This time I discovered the most furtive word, the least stressed, the weakest in English, a word which is not even a word, which barely sounds between the teeth, a breath, a mere nothing, the article *the*.[61]

With "a mere nothing" one of the most complex literary works of the twentieth century ends, only to begin again with the first line: "riverrun past Eve and Adam's . . ." (*FW*, 3.1).

In addition to the general structure, characters, and plots, it also helps to get a general sense of the "Wakean" language that Joyce worked with. As has already been pointed out in the previous chapters, Joyce the Irishman had an uneasy relationship with the English language that was complicated by centuries of British colonial rule in Ireland. If the English language was not his own, he went to great lengths to demonstrate how easily he could transform, deform, and, subsequently, control it. If he really was, as he once boasted, at the end of the English language with *Ulysses*, the creation of a new language seemed like the logical next step. With *Finnegans Wake* Joyce wanted to give his "vocabulary the elasticity of sleep" and unite as many languages as possible in a kind of Babelian stew: "All the languages are present, for they have not yet been separated. It's a tower of Babel . . . The history of people is the history of language."[62]

In trying to hear what Joyce is seeing, it will help if "you spigotty anglease" (*FW*, 16.6–7). *Finnegans Wake* is "basically English," but it is not the "plain English" that any native speaker might be used to (*FW*, 116.26, 124.19). Many of the words look familiar, and they are even arranged in sentences with syntax and adorned with punctuation. Anyone will recognize, for example, what "They lived und laughed ant loved end left" means when it is read aloud (*FW*, 18.19–20). A sentence like this is striking because the written words give us new ways to imagine the spoken sense. Getting the gist of an entire sentence is not always possible. Individual parts might seem familiar but they do not easily link up with what comes before and after. Sometimes you will have to content yourself with unpacking a single word or a sequence of words that have been torn apart, rewritten or sounded out with different spellings, and combined with other words (from an expansive lexicon of other languages). Through these playful language games, Joyce created new words and gave old words new meanings.

It is sometimes easier to figure out what a word means if you can make out the broader context. When there are combinations of words around a particular theme, the interpretive process can be thrilling. Here is one address to Tim Finnegan early on in Book I: "Hohohoho Mister Finn, you're going to be Mister Finnagain! Comeday morm and, O, you're vine! Sennday's eve and, ah, you're vinegar! Hahahaha, Mister Funn, you're going to be fined again!" (*FW*, 5.9–12). Each exclamation refers to Tim Finnegan, whose name appears as "Mister Finn," "Mister Finnagain," "Mister Funn" and "fined again." The first sentence is pretty straightforward and plays off the fact that the name Finnegan sounds like the two words "Fin" and "Again," which, as mentioned earlier, play off the words for end and beginning. The second sentence has some familiar and unfamiliar words, but when read in the light of the third sentence, more interpretative possibilities open up: "Monday morn and oh you're fine! Sunday eve and ah, you're vinegar." "Vine" sounds like "fine," but what does it mean to be "vinegar"? Vine and vinegar share an etymological connection (French "vin," Italian "vino," etc). If taken a step further, the vine could imply "ripe" and the vinegar "sour." There are a number of ways to read this passage, but the decoding process it requires is pretty much the same for the entire book. You will try to match up the literal and figurative meanings and find ways to create new meaning with them. Sometimes "vinegar" can refer to vine, wine, or "sour." At other times it can simply mean what it says: vinegar.

In preparing his material for *Finnegans Wake*, Joyce kept a series of notebooks in which he collected lists of words and phrases.[63] He would use these notebooks to generate or revise passages as he went along. A number of what Molly Bloom would call "plain words" can be found in the notebooks and the *Wake* itself, but Joyce assiduously worked with the portmanteau. Anyone familiar with Humpty Dumpty's definition from Lewis Carroll's *Through the Looking-Glass* will know that a portmanteau has two meanings packed up into one word.[64] The portmanteau is the most common word unit in *Finnegans Wake*. It follows the same formula as that established by Carroll but tends to exceed two meanings.

Every reader will come up with his or her favorite portmanteau. I am particularly fond of "astonaged," which sounds like "astonished" but is built from the words "a," "stone," and "aged." The word "bisexcycle," for instance, builds on the prefix "bi" and suggests the words "bisexual," "bisect," and "bicycle." This same word could also be broken down into three parts: "bi," "sex," and "cycle." A word like "funferall" follows the same logic: possible combinations include "fun" and "funeral" or a "fun-for-all" (*FW*, 13.15). Anna Livia's "loveleavest dress" looks like the "loveliest dress" or the "love leavest dress," which would seem appropriate for her since she is also the River Liffey collecting leaves as she courses through Dublin (*FW*, 624.22). Each word or sequence of words can generate a plurality of possible meanings. One does not take precedence over the other. Rather, the unexpected spellings and word combinations work together to create an entirely new linguistic universe. In the world of the *Wake*, a funeral can be a fun free-for-all (especially for Tim Finnegan's boisterous wake), and Anna Livia can have the "leaviest dress" that is also lovely.

In addition to the portmanteau, readers soon discover that puns are everywhere. "Such a book, all in puns!," Joyce exclaimed proudly to a friend.[65] Even Joyce himself was surprised by the success he had working with puns. In its most basic definition, a pun is a word (or multiple words) that plays off the sound or spelling of other words. Puns are generated when a word has two different meanings, when two words that are spelled differently sound the same, or when two words that sound or are spelled the same have different meanings. There are thousands of puns in *Finnegans Wake* that play off words that everyone will know: these include the days of the week, "Someday duly, oneday truly, twosday newly, till whensday" and the name of the author himself, "ghem of all jokes" and "Mr Jinglejoys" (*FW*, 457.19–20, 193.9, 466.18). Joyce also pays homage to his favorite authors "the divine comic Denti Alligator" (Dante Alighieri), "a nuncio" (D'Annunzio), a "homerole poet" (Homer), and "Shakehisbeard" (Shakespeare), and to the Italian Renaissance and Baroque painters "Bottisilly, Tittoretto, Vergognese, Coraggio, Mazzaccio" (Botticelli, Tintoretto, Veronese, Caravaggio, and Masaccio) (*FW*, 440.6, 445.26, 445.32, 177.32, 435.7–8). He concocted puns from a variety of languages and consulted all kinds of books, newspapers, dictionaries, and encyclopedias.

Part of "getting" a pun depends on what you know, where you are from, what language or languages you speak, and what you have read. If you do not know Triestine dialect, as Joyce did, you might miss the connection between "okey boney" and "o che boni" ("oh how good they are") (*FW,* 386.9).[66] Some puns are more obvious than others, but they are certainly there for everyone to enjoy even if it would be impossible to pick them all out. For Joyce, it was enough that his readers recognized what they could. To Jacques Mercanton, he explained that certain puns will be missed, but there is something for everyone:

> You are not Irish . . . and the meaning of some passages will perhaps escape you. But you are Catholic, so you will recognize this and that allusion. You don't play cricket; this word may mean nothing to you. But you are a musician, so you will feel at ease in this passage. When my Irish friends come to visit me in Paris, it is not the philosophical subtleties of the book that amuse them, but my recollection of O'Connell's top hat.[67]

Although some puns are easy enough to understand, others are wildly obscure and go overlooked (unless, of course, you decide to consult an annotated guide). During the revision process, Joyce sometimes intentionally complicated individual passages and once added Samoyed words when a passage was "not obscure enough."[68] In his diary Stuart Gilbert recounts one revealing instance when Joyce worked up puns from the five volumes of the *Encyclopedia Britannica*:

> He has made a list of 30 towns, New York, Vienna, Budapest, and Mrs. [Helen] Fleischman has read out the articles on some of these. I "finish" Vienna and read Christiania and Bucharest. Whenever I come to a name (of a street, suburb, park, etc.) I pause. Joyce thinks. If he can Anglicise the word, i.e. make a pun on it, Mrs. F records the name or its deformation in the notebook. Thus "Slotspark" (I think) at Christiania becomes Sluts' park. He collects all queer names in this way and will soon have a notebook full of them.[69]

From this experience, Gilbert skeptically concluded that Joyce's method was "too easy to do and too hard to understand."[70] Gilbert is right on some level: the composition of *Finnegans Wake* was often completely arbitrary, and many of the jokes, puns, allusions, and portmanteaus could make sense only to Joyce himself. But Gilbert also seems to have missed an even more significant point about how we can read and enjoy the *Wake*. As much as we are tempted to translate every word and pin down every last reference to a definite source, there is no master key that will unlock it.

Instead, these discoveries of each word and its possible references further our understanding of how Joyce worked and they enrich what we read. They do not, however, tell us how we should read. We will never arrive at an original "Anglicized" version because none exists. *Finnegans Wake* is not a translation. It is an entirely new language built from cultural circulations and exchanges that have taken place for thousands of years. As early as 1907, when he delivered his lecture on Ireland in Trieste, Joyce asked, "What race, or what language, can boast of being pure today?" (*CW*, 166). He waited another thirty-two years to publish an emphatic answer: none.

In *Finnegans Wake*, individual sentences, passages, and chapters often recapitulate themes, structures, and techniques woven throughout the entire book. Joyce believed, along with the poet William Blake whom he greatly admired, that art has the power to transcend time and space by telescoping the universal through the particular. Even a single word, if well chosen, can serve as the starting point for exploring, and sometimes explaining, the workings of this Wakean cosmos (at least part of it, anyway). The "Anna Livia Plurabelle" chapter (I.viii), which closes Book I and marks the arrival of night, is a particularly good place to see how this process of universalizing through the particular works. Joyce began writing "Anna Livia Plurabelle" in 1923, published extracts from it in 1925 and 1927, and published it as a separate deluxe edition in 1928. He continued to work on it throughout the 1930s, and collaborated on French, German, and Italian translations. By the time *Finnegans Wake* was published, "Anna Livia Plurabelle" had undergone a series of almost twenty revisions. Joyce was particularly fond of this chapter and often used its formal coherence and lyricism as a defense against his critics. One enthusiastic supporter told him that it "was the greatest prose ever written by a man!" (*LI*, 282).

In a letter to Harriet Shaw Weaver, Joyce described what he was up to:

> It is a chattering dialogue across the river by two washerwomen who as night falls become a tree and a stone. The river is named Anna Liffey. Some of the words at the beginning are hybrid Danish-English. Dublin is a city founded by Vikings . . . Her Pandora's box contains the ills flesh is heir to. The stream is quite brown, rich in salmon, very devious, shallow. The splitting up towards the end (seven dams) is the city abuilding. Izzy will later be Isolde (cf. Chapelizod). (*SL*, 302)

Joyce's outline makes the chapter seem easier to follow than it actually is on a first read. If you pick up "ALP," as he affectionately called it, without knowing what Joyce intended, it would take you a while to make out a river running, night falling, and a city abuilding. But with or without Joyce's explanation, you can see (or hear) for yourself that there is more than one person speaking as the chapter opens: "O, tell me about Anna Livia! I want to hear all about Anna Livia. Well, you know Anna Livia? Yes, of course, we all know Anna

Livia" (*FW*, 196.1–3). There are no quotation marks, 2/em dashes, or a third-person narrator to divide the conversation. But it does not take long before you can begin to separate the eager exclamations and questions of one voice from the self-assured answers of the other. At first the washerwomen restrict their gossip to HCE and his mysterious crime in Phoenix Park ("Fiendish Park"), but before long they focus on ALP and begin to make her "private linen public" (*FW*, 196.16).

Once you have the two gossipers more or less in place, and you know that they are talking about HCE and ALP, you need to figure out what they say. Before consulting the guidebooks or summaries, give yourself some time to discover the individual voices. It helps to read it aloud, and I definitely recommend getting hold of the recording of Joyce reading some excerpts. You will not catch everything they say, but with a little patience you will begin to pick out some of the themes, characters, and linguistic variations that have popped up earlier and will again. As much as "ALP" marks another progression in the book, it is also a digression, "the seim anew," revisiting what has already been said before (*FW*, 215.23).

This chapter is also a good place to explore how, as Samuel Beckett put it, "form *is* content, content *is* form."[71] Since ALP is the River Liffey (in Dublin), the language mimics the sounds that a river might make. In preparing this chapter, Joyce, then living in Paris far away from the Liffey, would often sit on the banks of the Seine to check if his prose was authentic enough. So far as I can tell, the "rivery" quality of the prose is another way of saying that it is "lyrical" and "alliterative." In addition to the river sounds, he also incorporated hundreds of river names from around the globe and liked to think that at some point in the future a little boy or girl from Tibet or Somalia might be surprised to discover his or her native river in the pages of his book (it is not clear if he was serious or not about this).[72] He managed to weave so many river names into this chapter (some claim that there are close to a thousand) that he joked to Harriet Shaw Weaver, "I think it moves" (*LI*, 259). In addition to the river sounds, the language later in the chapter describes one woman turning into a tree ("My foos won't moos. I feel as old as yonder elm" 215.34–35) and the other into a stone ("I feel as heavy as yonder stone" 215.36). As the river gets louder, they have a difficult time hearing each other: "Ho! Are you not gone ahome? What Thom Malone? Can't hear with the bawk of bats, all thim liffeying waters of" (*FW*, 215.32–34). As night falls and their metamorphosis continues, their conversation turns to the Earwicker brothers, Shem and Shaun.

In 1938, Joyce collaborated with his friend Nino Frank on an Italian translation of "Anna Livia Plurabelle." He was worried that if he waited too long, he would forget what he originally intended. "We must begin work before it's too late," he told Frank. "For the moment there is still one person in the world, myself, who can understand what I have written. I can't guarantee that in two or three years I will still be able to."[73] During their collaboration, however, Joyce quickly abandoned any attempt to find an exact translation of every word and instead began to play with the sound, meter, and rhythm afforded by the Italian language.[74] In the process of transforming his Irish "Plurabelle" into an Italian "Plurabella," sound took precedence over sense, and he devised dozens of Italian puns and references to replace the original Irish ones. For one, he translates the "wyerye rima" ("*rima*" is Italian for "rhyme") that ALP is said to have written into "*la torza rima*," or the "*terza rima*" rhyme scheme that Dante Alighieri invented for the *Divine Comedy* (FW, 200.33).[75] It is no surprise that the only word to go untranslated was the already Italianized phrase "Ordovico or Viricordo," which plays off the name of Vico (author of *New Science*) and "*vi ricordo*" (I remember you). The Italian "ALP" was the last thing Joyce wrote.

What Joyce did with the Italian translation of "ALP" is what we as readers do with the *Wake*. The words are there to be sounded out, played around with, and, when possible, arranged into a number of interpretative possibilities. Regardless of who you are, where you come from, and what language (or languages) you know, reading *Finnegans Wake* is a process of creative rereading, of finding ways to make the individual words open up to your own understanding of the world. If the *Wake* is universal, as so many have suggested, it is because the words, stories, and characters have antecedents in so many cultures around the globe. And maybe this is, after all, Joyce's greatest achievement. In writing *Finnegans Wake*, he created a literary work that it is impossible for any one reader to master and any single culture to claim as its own.

Chapter 4

Reception

1914–1941

Throughout his life James Joyce circulated newspaper clippings, book notices, and journal articles to friends and potential critics. They were a subtle solicitation for a review, a translation, or an essay about him and his work. Joyce's transition from struggling author to monumental literary figure happened, in part, because of his keen talent for tapping into an expansive print culture. It also helped that he was surrounded by a coterie of eager friends and acquaintances willing to promote him. Strains of this careful supervision of his public persona became noticeable during the Trieste decade when he was still struggling to get published. In one of his more amusing bids for recognition, he ordered Stanislaus to insert a paragraph in *Il Piccolo della Sera* announcing the opening of the Volta cinema that he arranged back in Dublin: "Go at once to Prezioso, show them [clippings from Dublin newspapers] and get a par: I nostri Triestini in Irlanda or like that. A little allusion to *me* and a little to the enterprise of the proprietors Edison and Americano (*without* giving their names) in opening here" (*LII*, 277). Complete with a byline, a title, a story, and a modest "little allusion," this blurb contains everything you could ask for in a newspaper article. For whatever reason, it never appeared.

Working as an occasional journalist himself, Joyce knew how to maneuver a "par" when necessary. Even after he left Trieste for Paris in 1920, he made sure that articles appeared in Trieste's newspapers announcing his international success. Self-promotion, for Joyce, was the shameless art of transference and translation. It was a method that Stuart Gilbert referred to disparagingly as "Joyce's fixed principle": "never act oneself, cultivate ostensible 'aloofness' and pull strings."[1] Although Gilbert was critical of this savvy form of networking, Joyce was convinced that he was merely "pushing [his] own wares" (*LI*, 104). After World War I distracted the public's attention from *Dubliners*, Joyce promoted his works with a vengeance. When *Portrait* was published in 1916, Harriet Shaw Weaver became the principal conduit for his recognition in Europe and America and arranged, when possible, to get reviews in the journals and newspapers he recommended. When in 1917 she suggested some foreign reviews that might advertise or review *Portrait*, Joyce responded, "A copy could be sent to Professor Federico Olivieri (professor of English literature), University of Turin, with notices also in the hope that he may notice it. This you might accompany by a diplomatic letter on your official notepaper" (*LI*, 103). Joyce's advice about the protocol for soliciting reviews is revealing. Notices breed other notices. Even the paper selection and the diplomatic tone can influence whether or not reviewers will agree to the request.

I begin with these early examples of Joyce "getting noticed" because they are indicative of a strategy he continued to use throughout the 1920s and 1930s as he attempted to shape his critical reception in Europe, England, and America. During these years, Joyce deliberately cast himself as a detached intellectual even though he laboured behind the scenes to promote his works. As evidenced by the attempted, though unsuccessful, censorship of *Dubliners* and the obscenity trials against *Ulysses*, Joyce did not shy away from the controversy surrounding his books. Rather, he invited it, believing that criticism of any kind could work as the surest form of publicity.

What follows is a broad survey of the critical reception that has sprung up in the past century or so to make sense of the man and his works.[2] It is roughly divided into two parts: the first examines Joyce's reception when he was still alive, and the second sketches the critical trends following his death. This sweep of Joyce's reception will give you an outline of the critical tradition and provide some possible areas for further research. Although the act of reading is a solitary activity, the act of interpretation is not. Over the years, Joyce has amassed an entourage of amateur and academic readers second only to Shakespeare or Dante, who, it should be added, had a significant head start. Some of the earliest and most perspicacious Joyce readers emerged without the mass of information that we have available to us now. For that reason, *Ulysses* looks very different today, for instance, from how it did to Stuart Gilbert when he wrote the first study of *Ulysses* in 1930. The list of readers and ways of reading continue to grow and change, and we are at a point now where the study of Joyce's life and works is a massive collaborative process supported by conferences, symposia, schools, institutes, and journals around the globe. How, when, and where you choose to read and reread Joyce is something that you will have to decide for yourself.

Ezra Pound was one of Joyce's earliest critics, supporters, and promoters at a time when he was still an unknown quantity. The numerous essays and reviews Pound wrote, particularly in the 1910s, defined how a number of influential critics would read Joyce for decades. In his first review of *Dubliners*, Pound developed an angle of interpretation from which he seldom deviated. He admired Joyce's realism as well as his "good clear prose," but he was quick to dissociate him from Irish writers involved in the Irish Literary Revival: "It is surprising that Mr Joyce is Irish. One is so tired of the Irish or 'Celtic' imagination (or 'phantasy' as I think they now call it) flopping about. Mr Joyce does not flop about. He defines. He is not an institution for the promotion of Irish peasant industries. He accepts an international standard of prose writing and lives up to it."[3] For Pound, the act of making Joyce "international" required downplaying his local, Irish influences. Joyce's writing, he believed, had more in common with Flaubert's realism than Yeats's mysticism. He continued the process of "de-Irishing" Joyce in another article appropriately titled "The Non-Existence of Ireland." "Joyce," he writes, "has fled to Trieste and into the modern world. And in the calm of that foreign city he has written books about Ireland."[4] As with his earlier review, Pound wanted readers to identify Joyce with a European literary tradition. He promoted Joyce as a quintessential modern writer capable of representing not a country but an "age." This cosmopolitan angle was something that Joyce encouraged as well.

In his subsequent reviews of *Exiles*, *Portrait*, and *Ulysses*, Pound continued to celebrate Joyce's cosmopolitanism. In 1922, one of his first public evaluations of *Ulysses* was an extended comparison between Joyce and Flaubert: "To begin with matters lying outside dispute I should say that Joyce has taken up the art of writing where Flaubert left it. In *Dubliners* and *The Portrait* he had not exceeded the *Trois Contes* or *L'Education*; in *Ulysses* he has carried on a process begun in *Bouvard et Pécuchet*."[5] Pound's early reviews and essays were pretty single-minded, but they presented Joyce as a supranational, European writer, one devoted to a universal human experience, not a nation or national literature. His writing belonged to the world of letters; he belonged to the world. Dramatic developments in contemporary literary theory in the 1970s and 1980s made it possible to recover the Irish contexts of Joyce's life and works that Pound and so many others downplayed.

T. S. Eliot offered another early and influential critical approach to Joyce. Although Eliot was not as prolific with his endorsements as Pound, he did offer a valuable way to read and understand *Ulysses*. In "Ulysses, Order, and Myth," published in *The Dial* in 1923, Eliot describes the "mythical method" that Joyce used to organize *Ulysses*. Not only does he emphasize the centrality of the *Odyssey* to the overall design of *Ulysses*, he argues that Joyce uses realism and myth to establish a link between "contemporaneity and antiquity":

> Mr. Joyce is pursuing a method which others must pursue after him. They will not be imitators, any more than the scientist who uses the discoveries of an Einstein in pursuing his own, independent, further investigations. It is simply a way of controlling, of ordering, of giving a shape and a significance to the immense panorama of futility and anarchy which is contemporary history.[6]

Eliot's essay sanctioned the contemporary relevance of Joyce's modern use of myth and presented the bulkiness of Joyce's novel, which seemed chaotic and unwieldy to the public, as a carefully constructed dialogue with a foundational text of Western literature. Entirely absent from Eliot's essay is a more basic discussion of the novel's plot, characters, or principal themes. Instead, he was interested in the fact that Joyce redefined the form and function of literature for an entire generation.

The essays of Pound and Eliot were central to the early reception of Joyce. At a time before the guidebooks and introductions were available, they identified some of the strange paradoxes of his writing: he was a realist who used a "mythical method," a novelist who exceeded the very limits of the novel form, an Irishman who belonged to Europe, and a universal writer obsessed with the local details of his native city (historical, geographical, social, and cultural). At the time, Pound and Eliot were interested in fashioning Joyce as an avant-garde, cosmopolitan artist. He did not belong to any of the literary movements then in vogue, but he was distinctly "modern."

By the end of the 1920s, when readers expressed confusion or hostility to the few sections of *Work in Progress* that appeared in the journal *transition*, Joyce was more proactive than usual. He collected twelve articles together in a single volume under the mock-scholarly title, *Our Exagmination Round His Factification for Incamination of "Work in Progress"* and told his friend Valery Larbaud, "I did stand behind those twelve Marshals more or less directing them what lines of research to follow" (*LI*, 283). The collection was brought out under Sylvia Beach's label Shakespeare and Company (the publisher for *Ulysses*) ten years before *Finnegans Wake* was published as a complete book.

Many of the contributors were Joyce's close friends, and in a series of spirited essays they explained that *Work in Progress* was a necessary step in his artistic development. In one of the more entertaining "exagminations," Samuel Beckett blamed the public for its inability to understand Joyce's latest literary experiment. Like the other contributors, he believed that Joyce was taking part in a more modern "revolution of language": "This writing that you find so obscure is a quintessential extraction of language and painting and gesture, with all the inevitable clarity of the old inarticulation. Here words are not the polite contortions of 20th century printer's ink. They are alive. They elbow their way on to the page, and glow and blaze and fade and disappear."[7] If the public had trouble making sense of *Work in Progress*, they would probably have had difficulty understanding Beckett's defense here. What does it mean to have words "elbow their way on to the page" anyway? Beckett also went on to explain that the language and form of Joyce's latest experiment belonged to an established literary and philosophical tradition. Giambattista Vico, he suggested, was central to the novel's design, and the distortions of the English language resemble what Dante did in the *Divine Comedy* when he standardized a number of Italian dialects.

Our Exagmination also includes essays by Stuart Gilbert and Frank Budgen, two of Joyce's friends who were called upon to write the first book-length studies of *Ulysses* in 1930 and 1934. As with Pound and Eliot, Gilbert and Budgen represent two ways of reading Joyce. For Gilbert, textual interpretation was a process of decoding the language and dismantling the structure before putting them neatly back together into a coherent system. His essay even contains a glossary intended to show newcomers how they might read and enjoy. Considerably less pedantic than Gilbert, Budgen believes that *Work in Progress* begins where *Ulysses* ends: "In *Ulysses* is the life – real life – of day; here the reality – super reality – of night."[8] More important to Budgen than the genius of Joyce is his humanity and unique power to represent the everyday and the divine, the real and the superreal, the conscious and the unconscious without giving precedence to either one.

Even to the most fanatical Joyceans, Gilbert oversystematizes his readings, sometimes stretching his evidence for a Homeric parallel or allusion beyond the realm of possibility. To the less fanatical, his obsessive desire for order has the tendency to take the fun out of reading. When he came to write *James Joyce's "Ulysses": A Study*, Gilbert carefully laid out the principal Homeric themes, characters, and parallels and used the "skeleton-key-summary-scheme" that Joyce gave him as the starting point for his episode-by-episode exegesis. In preparation for the task, he also reread Homer's *Odyssey* in the original Greek (even though Joyce had not).

Because *Ulysses* was still banned in England and America, Gilbert included lengthy quotations and provided step-by-step interpretations of both possible, and sometimes improbable, Homeric readings. He leaves little room for dissenting opinions and goes out of his way to align the copious details to a broader network of symbols. One passage describing Molly Bloom should suffice as an example: "She begins small, a very ordinary woman, the *petite bourgeoisie* of Eccles Street, a humbler Madame Bovary, to end as the Great Mother of the gods, giants and mankind, a personification of the infinite variety of Nature as she has developed by gradual differentiation from the formless plasma of her beginning."[9] Gilbert set in motion a reading practice that continued throughout the 1960s as critics attempted to synthesize every character, detail, and event into a universal archetype.

When Frank Budgen published his own study four years after Gilbert, *Ulysses* was still banned in England. In *James Joyce and the Making of "Ulysses,"* he combines biographical reminiscences with more straightforward critical explanations. Budgen knew Joyce in Zurich during World War I, and he brings Joyce's personality to bear on the evolution of *Ulysses*:

> Joyce's method of composition always seemed to me to be that of a poet rather than that of a prose writer. The words he wrote were far advanced in his mind before they found shape on paper. He was constantly and indefatigably in pursuit of the solution to some problem of Homeric correspondence or technical expression or trait of character in Bloom or another personage of "Ulysses."[10]

Budgen's book provides a number of informative readings of the plot, characters, and principal themes and provides us with rare glimpses into Joyce's workshop so that we can observe his methods of composition. To this day, it remains one of the great books about Joyce and *Ulysses*.

Joyce was always guarded about the public presentation of his private life, and he carefully monitored, and on occasion censored or revised, what others wrote about him. For his first biographer, Herbert Gorman, this kind of meddling proved to be a complete nightmare. Gorman's biography, which he began writing in 1930 hoping to publish it a year later, was intended to complement the publication of Gilbert's *Study*. The act of compiling information about Joyce's life was more onerous than Gorman initially expected: Joyce's friends and family were in distant cities he could not afford to visit, and Joyce was inconsistent with his support. After three years, the biography was still unfinished and Joyce withdrew his authorization (he later agreed to reauthorize it). When it was finally ready in 1938, Joyce urged Gorman to stall the publication so that *Finnegans Wake* could appear first.

Gorman's *James Joyce* offers a prim and proper portrait of the artist. Joyce is presented as a family man in a "comfortable velvet house-jacket." "No one," Gorman assures us, "has ever seen the real Joyce who has not seen him in the relaxed pleasantness of his own home."[11] Joyce read through the entire manuscript, and in a number of revisions and curious footnotes he played an active part in the making of his own myth: he was neglected by his native city, betrayed by his friends and family, and forced into a life of voluntary exile. He also settled some old scores or responded to rumors. In one particularly revealing footnote about his refusal to return to Ireland in the 1920s, he compares himself with Parnell: "Having a vivid memory of the incident at Castlecomer when quicklime was flung into the eyes of their dying leader, Parnell, by a chivalrous Irish mob, he did not wish a similar unfortunate occurrence to interfere with the composition of the book he was trying to write."[12] In addition to the footnotes, there are a number of revealing silences: Lucia's mental illness is never mentioned and few events in Joyce's life after 1922 are described. Gorman's Joyce is an elaboration of the supra-national artist championed by Pound and Eliot. He is an exceptional Irish-man, who inhabits the "international world of letters where national boundaries mean nothing at all."[13]

1941–2005

After Joyce's death in 1941, there was a shift from amateur interest to academic institutionalization. If he was once at the forefront of the European avant-garde, he was soon anchored in the American academy. His brother Stanislaus and many of his friends were still alive to put his life and works in order, but he was no longer around to influence his reception. He did, however, unwittingly influence who was chosen to write the first critical introduction to his works. In 1939 Harry Levin (an American professor of Comparative Literature at Harvard University) wrote an article on *Finnegans Wake* that still provides one of the best introductions for beginners. Joyce dispatched a letter thanking him, and with this vote of confidence the publisher selected Levin to write *James Joyce: A Critical Introduction* (1941) for its "The Makers of Modern Literature" series. Levin was also responsible for editing *The Portable James Joyce* (1946), which included expurgated selections and full text reprints of Joyce's oeuvre. His influence on Joyce's reception cannot be underestimated. His eloquent *Critical Introduction* garnered a wide readership and made Joyce respectable and accessible enough for college syllabi across America.

Without anyone peering over his shoulder, Levin was free to make his own critical judgments about Joyce's contribution to literary history. Written long before the flood of primary source material, biographies, and critical studies,

Levin's book is a remarkable achievement. He tackles each of Joyce's works individually and balances sophisticated readings with their broader formal and thematic implications. Levin also acknowledges Joyce's vexed relationship with his nation and national identity: "As for Joyce, his books could not and cannot be published or sold in his native country. They are of Irishmen and by an Irishman, but not for Irishmen; and their exclusion was Joyce's loss as well as Ireland's."[14] Written between 1940 and 1941 when Europe and America were embroiled in World War II, Levin's book acknowledges that the world to which Joyce belonged was on the verge of disappearing. For this reason, his introduction presents an artist strangely out of place in his world. If Pound and Eliot made him distinctly modern, Levin, disillusioned by the war like so many others, assessed what this process of becoming modern actually cost him. His introduction had the effect of making Joyce the ultimate twentieth-century humanist, a universal mind and self-appointed defender of culture and civilization.

In the 1950s two of Joyce's most influential critics emerged: Hugh Kenner and Richard Ellmann. Following Levin's example, both men wanted to continue making Joyce's work intelligible to a wider readership. They represent radically different approaches, and in a longlasting spat that continued through the 1980s, they marked out two poles of Joyce criticism. In 1956 Kenner published *Dublin's Joyce*. Unlike his predecessors, he was more familiar with Ireland and the Irish, and this informed the way he understood the language, characters, and contexts of Joyce's fiction. He was particularly keen to show that Joyce's ear was forever tuned to the language of Dublin and that from *Dubliners* to *Finnegans Wake* Joyce was always rummaging through a mass of materials he collected during his Irish-Catholic upbringing. Despite his scattered emphasis on the Irish contexts, Kenner still supported the Europeanization process begun by Pound.

In one of his more famous interventions, one very familiar today, Kenner dismissed the popular assumption that Stephen Dedalus was an autobiographical portrait of James Joyce as a young man. This identification between author and character, Kenner argued, was absurd since Stephen had serious emotional and intellectual limitations that would make it impossible for him to write something as replete with human pathos as *Ulysses*. Instead, he argued, the priggish and humourless Stephen belonged more with the James Duffys, Jimmy Doyles, and Gabriel Conroys of *Dubliners*. With this skeptical reading, Kenner made subsequent readers wary of treating Stephen without a strong sense of irony.[15]

Often opposed to Kenner's "antihumanist" irony is the work of Ellmann. In 1959 Ellmann published his monumental biography, *James Joyce*. It was his goal to provide a definitive account of Joyce's life. He not only introduces a wealth of previously unknown facts but also skillfully weaves them together into a coherent and entertaining narrative. Although no one would deny the greatness of Ellmann's achievement, there were a number of critics, including Kenner, who believed that he too often conflated the life with the fiction. It has also been suggested that Ellmann often sought coherence at the expense of accuracy.

Even before the biography was finished, Ellmann's friend Ellsworth Mason expressed serious reservations about the biographical sleights of hand he could pull off with his elegant prose style: "The trouble with your performances is that they have a kind of self-contained beauty of their own, and even in deepest error you have an intelligence of expression that is rare in Joyce criticism. I hereby predict that your errors about Joyce will be the last to depart from this earth."[16] In 1982, when Ellmann revised his biography, Kenner reviewed it for the *Times Literary Supplement* and made the case that *James Joyce* should not be deemed "definitive." Corrections continue to be made, but Ellmann's biography is still an indispensable resource for anyone interested in Joyce.

Kenner and Ellmann arrived when Joyce was known to most of the world by name only. Although they had more in common than both were perhaps willing to admit, their dispute represented two different ways to look at Joyce: there was the ironic realist or the humanist mythmaker. It was not long before these distinctions, tenuous as they were to begin with, were reconsidered after the various advances in contemporary theory (poststructuralism, feminism, psychoanalysis, Marxism, cultural studies, new historicism, and postcolonialism). From the late 1960s to the present, these critical approaches made it possible to read Joyce's life and works in new and exciting ways.

That there is an arena in which discussions and arguments could take place, then and now, was made possible by a handful of visionary critics, who established journals, local conferences, and international symposia devoted entirely to Joyce. In 1963 Thomas Staley, along with Fritz Senn (director of the James Joyce center in Zurich), founded the *James Joyce Quarterly*. The *JJQ*, as it is often called, made it possible for scholars from around the globe to share their research with one another. In 1967 Staley and Senn teamed up with Bernard Benstock and Zack Bowen to organize the first international Joyce symposium in Dublin, whose success inspired them to found an International James Joyce Foundation. These international symposia continue today, and they have been followed by a number of conferences, reading groups, and summer schools in Ireland, England, America, and Europe.

Although the goals of Staley, Senn, Benstock, and Bowen and others were at first modest, they are responsible for developing an infrastructure that anchored Joyce further in the academy. Since then, the "Joyce industry," as it is sometimes called, has developed into a global enterprise.

Joyce may have lived before deconstruction, but it was not long before critics discovered that his texts were "an apt testing ground and whetstone."[17] Margot Norris's *The Decentered Universe of "Finnegans Wake"* (1974) marks the first full-scale deconstructive reading of Joyce in English. In addition to exploring the unstable structure of the "dream language" of *Finnegans Wake*, Norris also considers how *Finnegans Wake* resists a linear narrative and defies readerly attempts to organize it within a traditional novelistic structure. By 1984 poststructuralist approaches were being continuously revised, adapted, and much discussed. In an effort to bridge the growing divide between French- and English-speaking audiences, Derek Attridge and Daniel Ferrer edited a volume entitled *Post-Structuralist Joyce*, which was comprised entirely of essays (many of them previously published in the 1960s) by leading French critics including Hélène Cixous, Jacques Aubert, and Jean-Michel Rabaté. Included among them was a contribution by Derrida himself, who acknowledged that he had been reading Joyce on and off for twenty-five or thirty years. Joyce's works, he admitted, played a part in his own ideas about deconstruction.

Emerging in conjunction with and in response to French and Anglo-American poststructuralism were a number of feminist approaches. Generally speaking, these various "feminisms" tended to have a different emphasis: the French feminists focused on the relationship between language and gender, American and British feminists concerned themselves with the literary text (plot, characterization, and setting), sometimes recovering female writers ignored by the canon or scrutinizing male representations of gender and sexuality. In 1984 Bonnie Kime Scott's *Joyce and Feminism* represented a major intervention in feminist and Joyce studies that opened up a number of other critical possibilities. She successfully combined rigorous theoretical investigations with original archival work that drew attention to the women in Joyce's life and in his fiction. Critics such as Karen Lawrence, Suzette Henke, Vicki Mahaffey, and Cheryl Herr used an eclectic blend of theoretical methodologies (psychoanalysis, Marxism, and deconstruction) to continue examining feminist issues. They pointedly asked questions that many of their male counterparts had not. What role did women play in Joyce's life? How does he represent women in his works? How did the patriarchal culture of Ireland impact on his writing? How does he play with the gendered constructions of language?

Feminist scholars made it abundantly clear that there were significant blindspots in our understanding of Joyce's life and works. Meanwhile, critical theorists of all stripes were consulting primary materials such as the three volumes of Joyce's letters (1957 and 1966) to see what else had been glossed over. In addition to the biographical revisions over the decades, archival material like the letters inspired a reevaluation of Joyce's interest in politics. In his effort to create a cosmopolitan Joyce, Ellmann, following the example of Pound and Gorman, emphasized his disinterest in politics, Irish or otherwise. By reading through the letters, particularly those written during the Trieste years, a number of critics soon came to believe that the image of an apolitical Joyce was no longer tenable. Such a reconsideration was also made possible by the belated publication of Joyce's early Triestine newspaper articles and Irish book reviews that were also edited by Ellmann and Mason and published as *The Critical Writings* in 1959 (the same year as his biography). Sources like the letters and the *Critical Writings* were evidence that Joyce's interest in Irish politics was more extensive and complicated than was at first thought.

Colin MacCabe's *James Joyce and the Revolution of the Word* (1978) was one of the first full-scale attempts to repoliticize Joyce. Working with theoretical concepts drawn from psychoanalysis (particularly Jacques Lacan), poststructuralism, and Marxism, MacCabe argues that Joyce's use of language was a radical attempt to challenge and dismantle forms of social and political power. Although Joyce refused to align himself publicly with Irish nationalist movements, MacCabe argues that his politics becomes manifest in the ways he deconstructs nationalist identifications and representations. Fast on the heels of MacCabe, Dominic Manganiello published *Joyce's Politics* (1980), a biographical and critical reassessment of the apolitical Joyce. Looking through the books and newspapers that Joyce read in Italy, Manganiello documents how Joyce's political opinions were decisively shaped by contemporary debates about Italian socialism and Irish nationalism.

This political turn influenced a broader investigation of Joyce's relationship with Irish language, history, literature, and culture. Spurred on by Edward Said's extremely influential book *Orientalism* (1978), a number of Irish writers and critics in the early 1980s began to examine Irish literature from a postcolonial perspective. It was Seamus Deane's work, in particular, that made the biggest impact in Joyce studies at this time. He reoriented the discussion of a political Joyce by emphasizing that his writing was itself a political gesture. For Deane, Joyce was not at home in Ireland, but it was precisely his geographical and psychological distance that enabled him to create and critique it. "The relationship between literature and politics,"

Deane contends, "was not . . . mediated through a movement, a party, a combination or a sect. For him, the act of writing became an act of rebellion; rebellion was the act of writing."[18] During the 1980s, the vexed question of Joyce's Irishness was also tackled by critics such as David Lloyd, Terry Eagleton, and Frederic Jameson, all intent on exploring the Irish historical and cultural contexts against which Joyce, paradoxically, both rebelled and defined himself.

From these interventions, critics in the 1990s set out to recover the centrality of Irish politics, history, and culture in Joyce. Enda Duffy's *The Subaltern "Ulysses"* (1994), Vincent Cheng's *Joyce, Race, and Empire* (1995), and Emer Nolan's *James Joyce and Nationalism* (1995) are some of the most notable examples. Although they often diverge in their arguments and conclusions, they have a vested interest in examining the role that imperialism, Irish literature, and nationalism played in Joyce's representations of Ireland and the Irish. Their work put an end to the longstanding acceptance that Joyce was an apolitical artist completely uninterested in Ireland's political debates and struggles.

Anyone who happens to glance at the Joyce shelf (or shelves) in a bookstore or library will find an extensive catalogue of guidebooks, annotations, and companions that have been compiled over the past sixty years or so to assist readers. Indeed, the list is extensive, and although these resources are intended to help readers along, they often have the opposite effect of overwhelming or intimidating them. Which is a shame, because this critical drive for collecting information emerged out of the desire to get a handle on Joyce's texts. These informational resources occupy a special place in the history of Joyce criticism because they have acted as a crutch for any and every reader unfamiliar with the thousands of musical, historical, popular, geographical, statistical, and literary references that pop up in Joyce's texts.

The information craze was officially kicked off by Richard Kain's *Fabulous Voyager* in 1947. Driven by a thirst for all kinds of empirical data, Kain unearthed and glossed hundreds of references contained in *Ulysses*. He scoured a number of the actual sources that Joyce used, including *Thom's Dublin Directory*, in an effort to compile everything from population statistics about turn-of-the-century Dublin to street and business addresses. Even if, as Kenner himself once wondered, Kain could not tell you why this information mattered, he established a longstanding critical tradition.[19] Building on Kain's example, Robert Adams published *Surface and Symbol: The Consistency of James Joyce's "Ulysses"* (1962). Unlike Kain, Adams sifted through the facts and divided them into categories of "symbols" and "surfaces": the former fit into a larger organizing principle, the latter serve as realistic ornamentation.

Adams was in search of a coherent structure for the novel built from the scraps of random facts (personal history, Dublin history, residential figures, and geography). The scholarly scavenging of Kain and Adams provided a valuable model for later critics, who wanted to synthesize the smaller details into a broader framework.

The search for all kinds of raw material in Joyce's works had two consequences: it emphasized that Joyce's fiction was built on a wealth of high- and low-brow pop-cultural and literary sources, and it proved just how much of the realism of his fiction was built from empirical details. Influenced by poststructuralist and Marxist approaches, a number of scholars began to examine the historical, social, and cultural contexts from which this information derived. In *Joyce's Anatomy of Culture* (1986), Cheryl Herr contends that the pop-cultural allusions in Joyce's texts address how "culture" shapes the consciousness of writer, character, and reader alike. From this central premise, Herr argues that the newspapers, theatrical productions, and sermons in Joyce's texts expose and challenge the cultural institutions (press, theater, Church) that define who and what we are. Her work inspired critics to begin looking at other cultural contexts that include such things as advertisements and popular fiction.

With its sophisticated theoretical analysis and original archival material, Herr's book became a model for scholars in the early 1990s eager to explore representations and theories of history. The impact of postcolonial studies and new historicism in the 1980s and 1990s triggered an interest in repressed or marginalized histories and a renewed desire to read historical accounts "against the grain." Because of its colonial past, Ireland was the perfect subject for scholars wanting to explore issues of historical representation, politics, language, and power in Joyce's works. James Fairhall's *James Joyce and the Question of History* (1993) and Robert Spoo's *James Joyce and the Language of History* (1994) represent two significant investigations. They argue that Joyce incorporated historical characters and events into his fiction, often revising them in the process, as a way to subvert the violence and oppression of Irish history and challenge more "official" historical interpretations. In addition, they complemented their analysis with archival sources that made it possible to flesh out the broader historical debates that were in circulation when Joyce was writing.

As theoretical approaches have gone in and out of vogue over the past five decades, a number of scholars have devoted themselves to editing, compiling, and collecting Joyce's manuscripts, notebooks, and loose memoranda. Many of these materials were relocated to a handful of American universities in the 1950s and 1960s or published in revised critical editions. Nevertheless, bits and pieces of Joyceana continue to pop up. A few years ago, an important collection of early drafts from *Ulysses* were found in an attic in Paris and bought by the National Library of Ireland for more than thirteen million dollars. For many people, tracking down someone's papers or deciphering his or her notes is far from interesting. But for Joyce readers, this archival work has provided a wealth of valuable information on the man and his method. Critics who have studied the manuscripts, notebooks, and drafts have been able to determine his writing habits, and they have decoded the various compositional stages, which enables us to better understand the genesis of Joyce's texts.

Just as deconstruction began to reach British and American academic circles in the early 1970s, a number of French scholars began to develop what they called "genetic criticism."[20] The genetic critics, many of them trained by these same French deconstructionists, wanted to identify the stages of composition within a given text from beginning to end. Particularly novel in their approach was the idea that each stage in the revision process represents a creative possibility or road not taken. For the French genetic critics, the individual work is not fixed. Rather, it represents one set of choices out of many.

In America, genetic criticism was confined primarily to an investigation of the compositional process with the goal of interpreting the text. Early critics like A. Walton Litz consulted the existing manuscripts for *Ulysses* and *Finnegans Wake* at the end of the 1950s in an attempt to find the "key" to Joyce's method. Although the "key" to the Joycean labyrinth eluded him (and still does for genetic critics today), he did discover that Joyce worked by a process of accretion, always adding and seldom subtracting as he revised. In 1977, when Michael Groden published *"Ulysses" in Progress*, he worked with the extant *Ulysses* manuscripts scattered around libraries and universities in England and America. In comparing them, he realized that they could be organized into a series of early, middle, and late stages. The experimental styles of each episode were part of a gradual process of discovery that Joyce developed as he moved along.

Between 1977 and 1979, the sixty-three volume *James Joyce Archive* was published, with Groden acting as the general editor. It contained black and white photographic reproductions of his manuscripts and notes without any editorial transcriptions. In the history of Joyce reception, the arrival of the *Archive* ranks high on the list of missed opportunities. Just at the moment when such a wealth of primary materials (including Joyce's notebooks, lectures, newspaper articles, and manuscript drafts) became available to a wider audience, very few scholars seemed to take notice. Joyce scholars were not entirely to blame. The cost for each volume was prohibitive and the supply extremely limited (250 hardback sets). Groden and his team created an invaluable resource for Joyce scholars that very few, save those with big checkbooks or access to a major resarch library, could get their hands on. At the end of the 1970s, contemporary theory was in its heyday, and genetic scholarship was kept in the critical closet.

In the mid-1980s, however, the issue of genetic criticism in Joyce studies resurfaced with a vengeance. Until this time, a number of *Ulysses* editions had been available, but they were all riddled with errors, some more serious than others. In an effort to establish a "definitive" text, Hans Walter Gabler, a German genetic critic, assembled the existing typesheets and manuscripts (including those reproduced in the *Archive*) and created a "copytext" that would serve as a foundation for his corrections (five thousand in all). Through a series of complex editorial decisions, Gabler and his team published a three-volume synoptic edition in 1984 that identified when and where Joyce added or deleted words and phrases. A single volume stripped of these notes was published in 1986.

It was this edition that sparked the "Gabler-Kidd controversy". Two years after the "corrected text" came out, another Joyce scholar named John Kidd published a scathing review, charging that Gabler had introduced more errors than he corrected. His initial condemnation was followed up with a 170-page investigation of these "errors." Kidd's attempt to discredit Gabler's edition inspired a flurry of critical responses. It was soon proven that the "errors" Kidd identified were largely incidental. Critics including Groden demonstrated that Kidd failed to consult the three-volume synoptic edition in which Gabler explained his editorial decisions. Kidd's case against Gabler was seen to have been way out of proportion and was soon dismissed. Regardless of the side critics chose to take, there was a general consensus that this new *Ulysses* was quite different from the one Joyce wrote. It corrected mistakes that Joyce may or may not have made and put Gabler in a position to decide what should and should not be corrected. Today it is largely agreed that Gabler's edition is the closest thing to a definitive text available. Readers past, present, and future, however, need to acknowledge that the *Ulysses* they have in hand is one version out of many.

Discussions about the indeterminacy of *Ulysses* continue, but much of the genetic attention has turned to the mass of materials that Joyce compiled when writing *Finnegans Wake*. Of particular interest are the forty-eight notebooks, which are currently being annotated by Vincent Deane, Daniel Ferrer, and Geert Lernout as part of the *"Finnegans Wake" Notebooks at Buffalo* project. *Finnegans Wake* poses significant challenges to genetic critics.

Although a great deal of work has been done since the 1940s to catalogue, gloss, and glean every word in the text, there has been a necessary turn back to the notebooks to account for the text's evolution. This next wave of genetic scholarship encourages the birth of a "genreader," who can approach *Finnegans Wake* through the mass of notebooks and manuscripts. For Jean-Michel Rabaté, this "genreader" will be "*genetic* in that (s)he . . . is always becoming, and transforming the text whose intentions are to be ascribed to a whole unstable archive, and *generic* because always poised in some sort of textual and sexual undecidability."[21] The act of reading through the archive, of looking at the notes that Joyce did and did not use, gives us a new way to think about the process of reading and writing. This "genreader" may, in fact, be the ideal reader Joyce had in mind: someone willing to approach every word in his work as a possibility.

Joyce readers have come a long way since 1914. At this moment there is a massive collection of primary and secondary materials that you can find in the library, at the bookstore, and on the internet. You may be interested in a particular critical or archival approach to Joyce, or you might just want to trudge through his works the old-fashioned way without any interference. Whatever you decide, you should know that Joyce keeps changing as the world does. If you decide to keep on reading and rereading him, you will discover that the rewards are well worth it. Coming back to his works after some time has passed is like meeting an old friend, one who can remind you where you have been and where, in the end, you might be going.

Notes

1 Life

1. Stanislaus Joyce, *My Brother's Keeper: James Joyce's Early Years*, ed. Richard Ellmann (New York: Viking, 1958), p. 108.
2. *Ibid.*, p. 128.
3. *Ibid.*, p. 164.
4. Joyce, *Brother's Keeper*, p. 192.
5. Willard Potts, ed., *Portraits of the Artist in Exile: Recollections of James Joyce by Europeans* (Seattle: University of Washington Press, 1979; New York: Harcourt, Brace and Jovanovich, 1986), p. 110. In *The Years of Bloom: James Joyce in Trieste, 1904–1920* (Dublin: The Lilliput Press, 2000), John McCourt assesses the full impact of this Trieste period and shows how much Joyce owed to the culture, politics, language, literature, and history of a town he happened upon almost by accident.
6. Noted in McCourt, *Years of Bloom*, p. 93.
7. Forrest Read, ed., *Pound/Joyce: The Letters of Ezra Pound to James Joyce*, (New York: New Directions, 1967), p. 24.
8. Silvio Benco, "James Joyce in Trieste," *Bookman* (New York), 72 (December 1930), pp. 375–80.
9. Potts, *Portraits*, p. 158.
10. Frank Budgen, *James Joyce and the Making of "Ulysses"* (1934; London: Oxford University Press, 1972), p. 191.
11. Noted in Herbert Gorman, *James Joyce: A Definitive Biography* (1941; New York: Rhinehart & Company, 1948), p. 143.
12. Read, *Pound/Joyce*, p. 159.
13. *Ibid.*, p. 196.
14. T. S. Eliot, *Selected Prose of T. S. Eliot* (New York: Harcourt, Brace & Jovanovich, 1975), p. 175.
15. Alan Travis, *Bound and Gagged: A Secret History of Obscenity in Britain* (London: Profile Books, 2000), p. 77.
16. *Ibid.*, p. 77.

2 Contexts

1. Quoted in McCourt, *Years of Bloom*, pp. 131–32.
2. For more extensive discussion of individual contexts, see Chapters 1, 2, 3, 4 and 11 in *The Cambridge Companion to James Joyce.*
3. Virginia Woolf, "Mr Bennett and Mrs Brown," in *The Essays of Virginia Woolf,* Volume III: *1919–24,* ed. Andrew McNeillie (San Diego: Harcourt Brace Jovanovich, 1986).
4. John Carey, *The Intellectuals and the Masses: Pride and Prejudice Among the Literary Intelligentsia, 1880–1939* (New York: St. Martin's Press, 1992).
5. Wyndham Lewis, *Time and Western Man* (Santa Rosa: Black Sparrow Press, 1993), p. 74.
6. Arthur Power, *Conversations with James Joyce,* ed. Clive Hart (London: Millington; New York: Columbia University Press, 1974), p. 78.
7. Virginia Woolf, *The Question of Things Happening: The Letters of Virginia Woolf,* Volume II: *1912–22,* ed. Nigel Nicolson (London: The Hogarth Press, 1976), p. 551.
8. Woolf, "Mr Bennett and Mrs Brown," p. 396.
9. Virginia Woolf, *A Writer's Diary* (New York: Harcourt Brace, 1954), p. 49.
10. Stanislaus Joyce, *Triestine Book of Days 1907–09,* 8 April 1907. Photocopies of the diary can be found in the Richard Ellmann collection at the McFarlin Library at the University of Tulsa.
11. Quoted in Potts, *Portraits,* p. 52.
12. Quoted in McCourt, *Years of Bloom,* p. 120.
13. Quoted in Giorgio Melchiori, "Joyce's Feast of Languages: Seven Essays and Ten Notes," *Joyce Studies in Italy* 4, ed. Franca Ruggieri (Rome: Bulzoni Editore, 1995), pp. 113–14.
14. McCourt, *Years of Bloom,* p. 238.
15. See my article "Getting Noticed: Joyce's Italian Translations," *Joyce Studies Annual* (2001), pp. 10–37.
16. Stanislaus Joyce, *Triestine Book of Days,* 5 May 1907.
17. For a full discussion of this lecture, see my article "On Joyce's Figura," *James Joyce Quarterly* 38: 3/4 (2001), pp. 431–51.
18. James Joyce, *Occasional, Critical, and Political Writings,* ed. Kevin Barry (Oxford: Oxford University Press, 2001), p. 179.
19. Joyce, *Occasional,* p. 174.
20. *Ibid.,* p. 176.
21. *Ibid.,* p. 171, emphasis mine.
22. Corinna del Greco Lobner, "A *Giornalista Triestino*: James Joyce's Letter to *Il Marzocco,*" *Joyce Studies Annual* (1993), p. 187.
23. Amalia Popper, *Araby* (Trieste: Casa Editrice Triestina, 1935).

3 Works

Dubliners

1. "James Joyce e Carlo Linati: Corrispondenza Inedita," *Inventario* 3 (1950), pp. 89–90.
2. *Dubliners* was originally twelve stories, but with the addition of "Two Gallants" and "A Little Cloud" it grew to fourteen, and with "The Dead" to fifteen.
3. John Wyse Jackson and Bernard McGinley, eds., *James Joyce's Dubliners: An Annotated Edition* (London: Sinclair-Stevenson, 1993), p. 10.
4. In his excellent Introduction to *Dubliners* (New York: Penguin, 1992), Terence Brown explores this idea; In *James Joyce: A Short Introduction* (Oxford: Blackwell, 2002), Michael Seidel expands on it.
5. See Margot Norris's suspicious reading of "Clay" in *Suspicious Readings Of James Joyce's "Dubliners"* (Philadelphia: University of Pennsylvania Press, 2003).
6. This phrase was coined by Michael Seidel.
7. This information is provided in Terence Brown's "Introduction" to *Dubliners*.
8. The circles in "Two Gallants," in fact, recall the various rectangles that circulate throughout "The Sisters." In addition to the lighted square of a window, we find grates, a card with a death announcement, an empty fireplace, a coffin with Father Flynn's "beautiful corpse," and a confession-box in which he is found laughing to himself.
9. *Dubliners* was originally supposed to end with "Grace." Joyce intended to parody the tripartite structure of Dante's *Divine Comedy* in which the pilgrim Dante moves from the Inferno to Purgatory before arriving in Paradise.

A Portrait of the Artist as a Young Man

10. The remaining chapters of *Stephen Hero* (16 through 26) were published separately in 1963.
11. Potts, *Portraits*, pp. 131–32.
12. If you are interested in the background material and contexts for *Portrait*, you should consult Robert Scholes and Rich and Kain, eds., *The Workshop of Daedalus: James Joyce and the Raw Materials for "A Portrait of the Artist as a Young Man"* (Evanston, Il: Northwestern University Press, 1966).
13. *Ibid.*, pp. 61–61.
14. *Ibid.*, p. 65.
15. In the "Oxen of the Sun" episode of *Ulysses*, Joyce uses nine English prose styles to parody the nine months of pregnancy. I suspect that this passage is a crude precursor: the word "fall" appears nine times and is intended to mark Stephen's symbolic rebirth. Is it another gestation parody? Maybe.
16. At one point Joyce imagined that he would write something on aesthetics. In 1903, when he was living in Paris, he wrote to his mother: "My book of songs will be published in the spring of 1907. My first comedy about five years later. My 'Esthetic' about five years later again (This *must* interest you!)" (*LII*, p. 38). The

"book of songs" would be *Chamber Music,* it is possible to see *Dubliners* or *Portrait* as a "comedy" of sorts the "esthetic" would never be written.

17. Forty epiphanies survive, but there were originally as many as seventy-one (maybe more).

18. Joyce used a series of notebooks that he kept in Paris (1902), Pola (1904), and Trieste (1907). You can find them reprinted in *The Critical Writings of James Joyce,* ed. Ellsworth Mason and Richard Ellmann (London: Faber and Faber; New York: Viking, 1959).

19. In putting this speech together, Joyce had in mind part of a letter that Gustave Flaubert wrote to a friend in 1852: "The author, in his work, should be like God in the universe, present everywhere and visible nowhere. Since art is a second nature, the creator of this second nature should employ similar methods." Quoted in Scholes and Kain, eds., *Workshop of Daedalus,* p. 247.

20. Budgen, "*Making of Ulysses*," p. 19.

21. Joyce regularly searched his brother's journals for literary material.

22. Hugh Kenner, *Dublin's Joyce* (1955; New York: Columbia University Press, 1987).

Exiles

23. Read, *Pound/Joyce,* p. 45.

24. *Ibid.,* p. 141.

25. *Ibid.,* p. 139.

26. "James Joyce e Carlo Linati," p. 89.

27. In the 1920s Linati would go on to translate some of Modernism's leading writers: Ezra Pound, Wyndham Lewis, Virginia Woolf, E. M. Forster, and Franz Kafka.

28. After receiving the commission, Linati was subsequently referred to in Joyce's letters as "the translator of *The Playboy of the Western World*" or the translator of "Synge and Yeats" (*LII,* pp. 447, 460).

29. Carlo Linati, "Ricordi su Joyce," *Prospettive* 2 (February 15, 1940), p. 16.

30. Carlo Linati, "Memorie a zig-zag," *La Fiera Letteraria* (1 January 1928), p. 1.

31. Carlo Linati, "James Joyce," *Il Convegno* (April 1920), p. 27.

32. Seidel, *Short Introduction,* p. 74.

33. In *Ulysses* Molly worries that she might be pregnant after sleeping with Blazes Boylan. She is relieved when her period comes.

34. The umbrella-contraceptive motif also surfaces in the very last line of *Giacomo Joyce* (London: Faber and Faber, 1968). The failed seduction by Giacomo of the nameless "she" is followed by an envoy: "Love me, love my umbrella" (*GJ,* p. 16).

Ulysses

35. Georges Borach, "Conversations with James Joyce," trans. Joseph Prescott, *College English* 15 (March 1954), p. 325.

36. Potts, *Portraits,* p. 131.

37. Why the Latin "Ulysses" for the title? Joyce's decision to give his book the Latin Ulysses instead of the Greek Odysseus was a distancing strategy that brought the

story of Ulysses away from a single origin. Moreover, as Joyce himself well knew, the story of Ulysses circulated outside of Greece and was continued by Joyce's other hero, Dante, who put the aged Ithacan in Hell for daring to travel past the pillars of Hercules and into the Southern Hemisphere. In choosing one of the earliest known literary works as his foundation, Joyce was also showing off. He knew that it would be almost impossible for future generations to think about Homer's Odyssey without thinking also of Joyce's *Ulysses*.

38. Louis Gillet, *Claybook for James Joyce* (London: Abelard-Schuman, 1958), p. 110.
39. A systematic reading of these geographical parallels can be found in Michael Seidel's *Epic Geography* (Princeton: Princeton University Press, 1976).
40. Seidel, *Short Introduction*, p. 88.
41. Read, *Pound/Joyce*, p. 145.
42. Stephen's parable may well be a missing story from *Dubliners*, and it is even accompanied by the perfect title in the form of a headline: "Dear Dirty Dublin" (*U*, 7: 921). Later in the day, Bloom associates his own cuckolding with plums: "He gets the plums and I the plumstones" (*U*, 13: 1098–99).
43. Georg Simmel, "The Metropolis and Mental Life," in *The Sociology of Georg Simmel*, trans. and ed. Kurt Wolff (London: Collier-Macmillan, 1950), pp. 410–11.
44. Potts, *Portraits*, p. 208.
45. In "Nausikaa" Bloom notices that his watch stopped at 4.30 p.m.: "Funny my watch stopped at half past four. Dust. Shark liver oil they use to clean. Could do it myself. Save. Was that just when he, she? O, he did. Into her. She did. Done. Ah!" (*U*, 13: 846–49).
46. Hugh Kenner has argued that Molly misinterpreted Bloom's words as he was falling asleep. She hears "eggs in the morning," but Bloom, Kenner thinks, was speaking gibberish.

Finnegans Wake
47. Potts, *Portraits*, p. 229.
48. The 1999 Penguin edition of *Finnegans Wake* also includes a spirited and brilliant introduction by John Bishop that you may find helpful.
49. Potts, *Portraits*, p. 132.
50. *Ibid.*, p. 237.
51. Harry Levin, *James Joyce: A Critical Introduction* (1941; New York: New Directions, 1960), p. 140.
52. Samuel Beckett et al., *Our Exagmination Round His Factification For Incamination of "Work in Progress"* (1929; New York: New Directions, 1972), p. 45. If Joyce had lived to write another book, there is some evidence to suggest that it would have been organized around the idea of an "awakening" and the sea.
53. Derek Attridge, "*Finnegans Wake*, or, The Dream of Interpretation," in *Joyce Effects: On Language, Theory, and History* (Cambridge: Cambridge University Press, 2000), pp. 133–55.
54. Read, *Pound/Joyce*, p. 228.

55. Potts, *Portraits*, p. 179.
56. *Ibid.*, p. 213
57. Joyce claimed that Vico was important for the creative process, but he discouraged people from looking too much into it: "I would not pay overmuch attention to these theories, beyond using them for all they are worth, but they have gradually forced themselves on me through circumstances of my own life" (*LI*, p. 241).
58. Joyce did not break *Finnegans Wake* into book or chapter titles. Readers have done this for the sake of convenience
59. There are nine more, though the last one has 101 letters.
60. Potts, *Portraits*, p. 149.
61. *Ibid.*, p. 197.
62. *Ibid.*, p. 207.
63. Those interested in the notebooks should check out the forty-eight *"Finnegans Wake" Notebooks* ed. Vincent Deane, Daniel Ferrer, and Geert Lernout, which are in the process of being annotated and republished (Belgium: Brepols, 2002).
64. Joyce claimed that he read Lewis Carroll's books only after he began *Finnegans Wake*. If you read the "Jabberwocky" poem, it is very hard to believe him.
65. Potts, *Portraits*, p. 198.
66. I owe this Triestine insight to John McCourt.
67. Potts, *Portraits*, p. 234.
68. *Ibid.*, p. 214.
69. Stuart Gilbert, *Reflections on James Joyce: Stuart Gilbert's Paris Journal*, ed. Thomas Staley and Randolph Lewis (Austin: University of Texas Press, 1993), pp. 20–21.
70. *Ibid.*, p. 21.
71. Beckett et al., *Exagmination*, p. 14.
72. Quoted in Danis Rose and John O'Hanlon, *Understanding "Finnegans Wake": A Guide to the Narrative of James Joyce's Masterpiece* (New York and London: Garland Publishing, 1982), p. 114.
73. Potts, *Portraits*, p. 96.
74. Ettore Settani, "Nota su *Finnegans Wake,*" *Prospettive* 4:2 (15 February 1940), p. 12.
75. For the Italian version, you should consult James Joyce, *Poesie e Prose*, ed. Franca Ruggieri (Milan: Mondadori, 1992), pp. 725–43.

4 Reception

1. Gilbert, *Reflections on James Joyce*, ed. Staley and Lewis, p. 45.
2. For a more extensive history of Joyce's critical reception, you should consult Joseph Brooker's *Joyce's Critics: Transitions in Reading and Culture* (Madison WI: University of Wisconsin Press, 2004).

3. Ezra Pound, *Literary Essays of Ezra Pound*, ed. T. S. Eliot (New York: New Directions, 1968), pp. 400–01.
4. *Ibid.*, p. 32
5. Read, *Pound/Joyce*, p. 194.
6. T. S. Eliot, *Selected Prose of T. S. Eliot*, ed. Frank Kermode (New York: Farrar, Straus and Giroux, 1975), p. 177.
7. Becket et al., *Exagmination*, pp. 15–16.
8. *Ibid.*, p. 45.
9. Stuart Gilbert, *James Joyce's "Ulysses": A Study* (1930; New York: Random House, 1955), p. 403.
10. Frank Budgen, *James Joyce and the Making of "Ulysses"* (1934; repinted London: Oxford University Press, 1972), p. 171.
11. Gorman, *Definitive Biography*, p. 339.
12. *Ibid.*, p. 217.
13. *Ibid.*, p. 337.
14. Levin, *Critical Introduction*, p. 6.
15. Kenner, *Dublin's Joyce*, p. xii.
16. Noted in Joseph Kelly's "Stanislaus Joyce, Ellsworth Mason, and Richard Ellmann: The Making of *James Joyce*," *Joyce Studies Annual* 3 (1992), p. 112.
17. Derek Attridge, *Joyce Effects: On Language, Theory, and History* (Cambridge: Cambridge University Press, 2000), p. 8.
18. Seamus Deane, "Joyce and Nationalism," in *Celtic Revivals: Essays in Modern Irish Literature 1880–1980* (London: Faber and Faber, 1985), p. 99.
19. Kenner, *Dublin's Joyce*, p. xi.
20. Michael Groden, "Genetic Joyce," in Jean-Michel Rabaté, ed., *Palgrave Advances in James Joyce Studies* (London: Palgrave, 2004), pp. 239–40.
21. Jean-Michel Rabaté, *James Joyce and the Politics of Egoism* (Cambridge: Cambridge University Press, 2001), p. 207.

Further reading

I have compiled an abbreviated list of book-length studies about Joyce's life, contexts, works, and reception. Full citations for any of the books I mentioned in Chapter 4 can be found below. For a more extensive list, you should consult the guide to further reading at the end of *The Cambridge Companion to James Joyce* (2nd edn., 2004).

Adams, Robert. *Surface and Symbol: The Consistency of James Joyce's "Ulysses."* New York: Oxford University Press, 1962.

Attridge, Derek, ed. *The Cambridge Companion to James Joyce*, 2nd edn. Cambridge: Cambridge University Press, 2004.

and Ferrer, Daniel, ed. *Post-Structuralist Joyce.* Cambridge: Cambridge University Press, 1984.

Beckett, Samuel et al. *Our Exagmination Round His Factification For Incamination of "Work in Progress"* (1929). Reprinted London: Faber and Faber; New York: New Directions, 1972.

Blamires, Harry. *The Bloomsday Book* (1966). Reprinted London: Methuen, 1985.

Brown, Richard. *James Joyce and Sexuality.* Cambridge: Cambridge University Press, 1985.

Budgen, Frank. *James Joyce and the Making of "Ulysses"* (1934). Reprinted London: Oxford University Press, 1972.

Campbell, Joseph and Robinson, Henry Morton, ed. *A Skeleton Key to "Finnegans Wake."* London: Faber and Faber, 1947.

Cheng, Vincent. *Joyce, Race, and Empire.* Cambridge: Cambridge University Press, 1995.

Deane, Seamus. *A Short History of Irish Literature.* London: Hutchinson; Notre Dame, IN: University of Notre Dame Press, 1986.

Deming, Robert H., ed. *James Joyce: The Critical Heritage*, 2 vols. London: Routledge, 1970.

Duffy, Enda. *The Subaltern "Ulysses."* Minneapolis: University of Minnesota Press, 1994.

Ellmann, Richard. *James Joyce* (1959). Reprinted Oxford: Oxford University Press, 1982.

Fairhall, James. *James Joyce and the Question of History.* Cambridge: Cambridge University Press, 1993.

Fargnoli, Nicholas A. and Gillespie, Michael P., ed. *James Joyce A–Z: The Essential Reference to His Life and Writings*. Oxford: Oxford University Press, 1995.

Gifford, Don. *Joyce Annotated: Notes for "Dubliners" and "A Portrait of the Artist as a Young Man."* Berkeley: University of California Press, 1982.

"Ulysses" Annotated. Berkeley: University of California Press, 1989.

Gilbert, Stuart. *James Joyce's "Ulysses"* (1930). Reprinted London: Faber and Faber, 1952; New York: Random House, 1955.

Gorman, Herbert. *James Joyce: A Definitive Biography* (1941). Reprinted New York: Rhinehart & Company, 1948.

Groden, Michael. *"Ulysses" in Progress*. Princeton: Princeton University Press, 1977.

gen. ed. *The James Joyce Archive*. 63 vols. New York and London: Garland Publishing, 1977–79.

Hart, Clive, ed. *A Concordance to "Finnegans Wake"* (1963). Reprinted Mamaroneck, NY: Paul P. Appel, 1973.

and Hayman, David, ed. *James Joyce's "Ulysses": Critical Essays*. Berkeley: University of California Press, 1974.

and Gunn, Ian. *James Joyce's Dublin: A Topographical Guide to the Dublin of "Ulysses."* London: Thames & Hudson, 2004.

Herr, Cheryl. *Joyce's Anatomy of Culture*. Urbana: University of Illinois Press, 1986.

Joyce, Stanislaus. *My Brother's Keeper: James Joyce's Early Years*, ed. Richard Ellmann. New York: Viking, 1958.

Kain, Richard. *Fabulous Voyager: James Joyce's "Ulysses."* Chicago: University of Chicago Press, 1947.

Kenner, Hugh. *Dublin's Joyce* (1956). Reprinted New York: Columbia University Press, 1987.

Levin, Harry. *James Joyce: A Critical Introduction* (1941). Reprinted New York: New Directions, 1960.

Litz, A. Walton. *The Art of James Joyce: Method and Design in "Ulysses" and "Finnegans Wake"* (1961). Reprinted London: Oxford University Press, 1964.

MacCabe, Colin. *James Joyce and the Revolution of the Word*. London: Macmillan Press, 1978.

Maddox, Brenda. *Nora: A Biography of Nora Joyce*. London: Hamish Hamilton; Boston: Houghton Mifflin, 1988.

Manganiello, Dominic. *Joyce's Politics*. London: Routledge, 1980.

McCourt, John. *The Years of Bloom: James Joyce in Trieste, 1904–1920*. Dublin: The Lilliput Press, 2000.

Nolan, Emer. *James Joyce and Nationalism*. New York: Routledge, 1995.

Norris, Margot. *The Decentered Universe of "Finnegans Wake."* Baltimore: Johns Hopkins University Press, 1974.

Potts, Willard, ed. *Portraits of the Artist in Exile: Recollections of James Joyce by Europeans*. Seattle: University of Washington Press, 1979; New York: Harcourt, Brace & Jovanovich, 1986.

Rabaté, Jean-Michel. *James Joyce, Authorized Reader.* Baltimore: Johns Hopkins University Press, 1991.

Read, Forrest, ed. *Pound/Joyce: The Letters of Ezra Pound to James Joyce with Pound's Essays on Joyce.* New York: New Directions, 1967.

Scott, Bonnie Kime. *Joyce and Feminism.* Bloomington: Indiana University Press; Brighton: Harvester, 1984.

Seidel, Michael. *James Joyce: A Short Introduction.* Oxford: Blackwell, 2002.

Senn, Fritz. *Joyce's Dislocutions,* ed. John Paul Riquelme. Baltimore: Johns Hopkins University Press, 1984.

Spoo, Robert. *James Joyce and the Language of History: Dedalus's Nightmare.* New York: Oxford University Press, 1994.

Index

Bulson, Eric.

The Cambridge
    introduction to
James Joyce.

3/09

$21.99

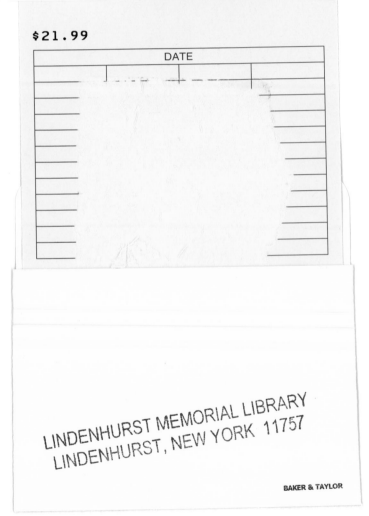

DATE		